Endowed

WITH

POWER

Endowed

WITH
POWER

HOW TEMPLE SYMBOLS
GUIDE US TO CHRIST'S
ATONEMENT

C. ROBERT LINE

CFI
An Imprint of Cedar Fort, Inc.
Springville, Utah

© 2017 C. Robert Line
Cover photos by Scott Jarvie
Photo credit:
    Andrew Bossi: 102 (left)
    Joshua Michael Gray: 6, 13, 14 (bottom), 16 (top)
    Library and Archives Canada: 103
    Line Family: 14 (top), 15 (bottom)
    Nicholas and Yin-Ying Sushkin: 15 (top)
    Sailko: 102 (right)
All rights reserved.

This is not an official publication of The Church of Jesus Christ of Latter-day Saints. The opinions and views expressed herein belong solely to the author and do not necessarily represent the opinions or views of Cedar Fort, Inc. Permission for the use of sources, graphics, and photos is also solely the responsibility of the author.

ISBN 13: 978-1-4621-2072-7

Published by CFI, an imprint of Cedar Fort, Inc.
2373 W. 700 S., Springville, UT 84663
Distributed by Cedar Fort, Inc., www.cedarfort.com

LIBRARY OF CONGRESS CATALOGING-IN-PUBLICATION DATA

Names: Line, C. Robert, author.
Title: Endowed with power : how temple symbols guide us to Christ's atonement
    / C. Robert Line.
Description: Springville, Utah : CFI, an imprint of Cedar Fort, Inc., [2017]
    | Includes bibliographical references and index.
Identifiers: LCCN 2017022454 (print) | LCCN 2017027203 (ebook) | ISBN
    9781462128242 (ebook) | ISBN 9781462120727 (pbk. : alk. paper)
Subjects: LCSH: Mormon temples. | Temple endowments (Mormon Church) |
    Atonement--Church of Jesus Christ of Latter-day Saints. | Church of Jesus
    Christ of Latter-day Saints--Doctrines. | Mormon Church--Doctrines.
Classification: LCC BX8643.T4 (ebook) | LCC BX8643.T4 L56 2017 (print) | DDC
    246/.9589332--dc23
LC record available at https://lccn.loc.gov/2017022454

Cover design by Shawnda T. Craig
Cover design © 2017 by Cedar Fort, Inc.
Edited and typeset by Kaitlin Barwick

Printed in the United States of America

10 9 8 7 6 5 4 3 2

Printed on acid-free paper

Many individuals were helpful in the production of this work. I would like to give special thanks to Michael Preece, Steve Schank, Ed Pinegar, John Peterson, and my wonderful wife, Tami—for their time, suggestions, encouragement, and direction. I am also grateful for and indebted to my brother Dan who spent countless hours with me in discussions about the topics contained within these pages. His interest and devotion to temples and temple worship gave me the courage to pursue this project. I also wish to give thanks to some wonderful spiritual, scriptural, and scholarly mentors in my life who have helped me to see, love, and appreciate the doctrine of the Atonement of Jesus Christ: Robert Millet, Kelly Haws, Rand Packer, and Grant Anderson. I would also like to thank the entire team at Cedar Fort Publishing for helping this book come to fruition.

Also by

C. Robert Line

Understanding the Doctrine of God's Time

*Pure Before Thee: Becoming Cleansed and
Changed by Christ*

Parables of Redemption

Contents

Introduction

*And daily in the temple . . . they ceased not to teach and
preach Jesus Christ. (Acts 5:42)*

One of my favorite duties as an LDS bishop was to organize, facili-
tate, and teach temple preparation classes. I learned many things
in those classes, and I am sure, or at least hopeful, that participating
ward members did too. One of the greatest things I learned was this:
The best temple prep class isn't a temple prep class at all. The best temple
prep class is the scriptures! To be fair, these classes do serve a wonderful
and practical purpose: they primarily prepare people to *enter* the temple;
but in my experience, they do not necessarily prepare one to be *in* the
temple. There is a difference. The temple is a place of visual and spiritual
beauty. Unfortunately, some Latter-day Saints are not always able to see
or feel this.

Over the years, I have been intrigued with the number of faithful,
believing Latter-day Saints who have struggled with certain aspects of the
temple, especially the endowment and its preliminary step of the initiatory
ordinances. Both in my roles as bishop and as a Church educator, I have
been intrigued with the number of faithful members who have expressed
to me their confusion and concern with regards to their attempts to deal
with, to reconcile, and to accept temple rituals and teachings. Several felt
they were not ready the first time they went for their endowment, even
though they participated in temple preparation courses and had studied

associated pamphlets and reading materials. Others have felt they are still not prepared and even a little bit in the dark, so to speak. My experience has shown me that these individuals are neither skeptics nor scorners, they are not doubters nor disloyal, they are not antagonistic nor atheistic; but almost without fail, I find they are all faithful seekers after truth. They hunger for knowledge, sacred knowledge, but all too often leave the temple with more questions than answers. Some have struggled with certain symbolic gestures or esoteric teachings. Some have said they find the temple endowment to be flat out strange or unusual. In an odd way, this is part of the reason I personally love the temple. These questionable quirks and interesting incongruities are what give the temple, at least for me, an air of authenticity. There is something genuine and real about these puzzling peculiarities and divine idiosyncrasies we encounter in temple worship. C. S. Lewis put it this way:

> Reality, in fact, is usually something you could not have guessed. That is one of the reasons I believe in Christianity. It is a religion you could not have guessed. If it offered us just the kind of universe we had always expected, I should feel we were making it up. But, in fact, it is not the sort of thing anyone would have made up. It has just that queer twist about it that real things have. So let us leave behind all these boys' philosophies—these over-simple answers. The problem is not simple and the answer is not going to be simple either.[1]

Another difficulty I have noticed is that some Church members, especially at the local levels, act as though we cannot talk about anything in the temple; we often hear this saying: "the temple isn't secret—it's sacred." Well, that may be true, but culturally we often treat God's holy house as though it is secret as well! The fact is we can talk about a lot of things, and many facets of temple worship can be found in the scriptures. Many things, especially in the endowment, have been taught openly by Church leaders, including those in the highest quorums of the Church. President Ezra Taft Benson observed: "Because of its sacredness we are sometimes reluctant to say anything about the temple to our children and grandchildren. As a consequence, many do not develop a real desire to go to the temple, or when they go there, they do so without much background to prepare them for the obligations and covenants they enter into." He then said: "I believe a proper understanding or background will immeasurably help prepare our youth for the temple."[2]

The only things we do not talk about are those specific things which we covenant not to discuss or reveal. But these are relatively few in number. Furthermore, the Lord does not instruct us to never talk of sacred things, only to take care when we do: "Remember that *that which cometh from above is sacred, and must be spoken with care, and by constraint of the Spirit; and in this there is no condemnation*, and ye receive the Spirit through prayer; wherefore, without this there remaineth condemnation" (D&C 63:64; emphasis added).

The purpose and intent of this book is to offer help to those struggling to make sense of certain puzzling aspects that they encounter in the temple. It is also to help expand the knowledge and appreciation for those who already feel a deep love for the temple, who do not necessarily struggle as some we have described. My hope is to accomplish this in a simple and singular way. No doubt there are other wonderful and informative books on the temple. This one serves a very specific and needed purpose—to point us to Christ and His infinite Atonement. Each chapter herein will have this goal. Other LDS temple books, of which there are many, are magnificent and often focus on very intricate and elaborate architectural designs or relevant and tantalizing historical and cultural motifs relating to the temple. We will look at a few of these aspects in this book too, but with the intent *to look to Christ*. Other temple books have been written with exclusive focus on ordinances and covenants in all their elaborate performances. This book will do that too, but just enough *to point us to Christ*.

I hope this book will highlight some other areas that have not been fully discussed, yet are very needful, and I believe it will help people not only prepare to *go* to the temple but to be *in* it as well. President David O. McKay once said, "Brothers and sisters, I believe that there are few, even temple workers, who comprehend the full meaning and power of the temple endowment. . . . If our young people could but glimpse it, it would be the most powerful spiritual motivation of their lives."[3] I agree with President McKay. My hope is that this book will serve as a simple yet sublime resource to enrich and enliven the worship experience that Church members can and should expect when they attend the House of the Lord. Elder L. Lionel Kendrick once stated: "There is a difference in just attending the temple and having a rich spiritual experience. The real blessings of the temple come as we enhance our temple experience. To do so, we must feel a spirit of reverence for the temple and a spirit of worship."[4] This is so true and we will certainly do this as we see the connection our temple worship has with the infinite Atonement of our Savior, Jesus Christ. This book is a personal endeavor and is not intended to represent the official teachings of the Church of Jesus Christ of Latter-day Saints.

Notes

1. C. S. Lewis, *Mere Christianity*, rev. ed. (1952; repr., New York: HarperOne, 2015), 42–43.
2. Ezra Taft Benson, "What I Hope You Will Teach Your Children about the Temple," *Ensign*, August 1985, 6.
3. David O. McKay in Truman G. Madsen, "House of Glory," BYU Ten-Stake Fireside address, March 5, 1972, 7.
4. L. Lionel Kendrick, "Enhancing Our Temple Experience," *Ensign*, May 2001, 78.

One

The Temple as a Symbol of Christ

*The temple is the house of the Lord. The basis for every temple
ordinance and covenant . . . is the Atonement of Jesus
Christ. Every activity, every lesson, all we do in the
Church, point to the Lord and His holy house.*
—*Russell M. Nelson*[1]

Often we say that temples are about families. Well, to be sure, we do things *as* families there, and we do things *for* families in the temple—but the family is not the *central* focus of the temple. The central focus is Christ, and we must not forget this vital aspect of the temple. President Boyd K. Packer once stated that the Atonement "is the very root of Christian doctrine." He went on to say, "You may know much about the gospel as it branches out from there, but if you only know the branches and those branches do not touch that root [the Atonement], if they have been cut free from that truth, there will be no life nor substance nor redemption in them."[2] So it is that the temple will have no life in its meaning nor purpose in its application to our lives unless we can see and understand its connection to and with the Atonement of Jesus Christ. Fortunately, there are multitude of reminders, many of them symbolic, that the temple and its associated system of ordinances gives us to help us remember this sacred and vital truth.

The Temple and the Big Dipper

One such example of the temple's focus on Christ and His infinite Atonement can be found in an interesting, yet obscure, stone relief on the west central spire of the Salt Lake Temple. Perhaps you have not noticed it before, but there you will find etched in stone the constellation of the Big Dipper! For those who have never noticed this before, it may seem a little bit odd. But the reason for its presence on the side of the temple can readily be seen and understood when one considers some practical purposes that this famous constellation served for ancient travelers and seafarers.

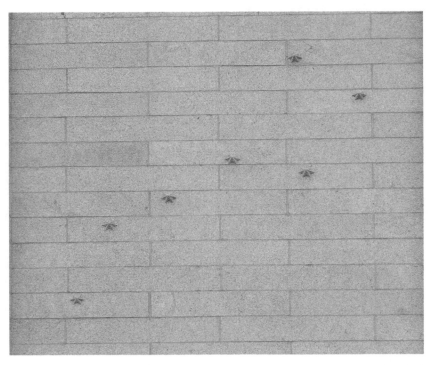

Big Dipper on the Salt Lake Temple

The two stars on the outer edge of the bowl of the Big Dipper point directly to the North Star, also called the Pole Star or Polaris. The earth's axis rising from the north pole points almost exactly to this famous star.

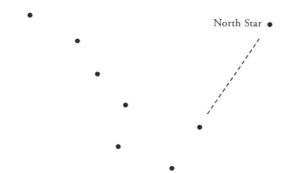

North Star

All other stars in the night sky seemingly revolve around this fixed point, which points the true way north. The value of this stellar arrangement lies in the fact that it allowed travelers anciently to be able to navigate, to plot a sure course toward their destination. Even if the North Star is covered in clouds, one could still use the constellation of the Big Dipper (if visible) to navigate and thus find one's way home.

So why did the early brethren of this dispensation choose to put an artistic depiction of the Big Dipper on the side of the Salt Lake Temple? Simply put, the temple is like the Big Dipper. Just as the Big Dipper points to the fixed point of the North Star, the star around which all other stars revolve, so does the temple point us to Him around whom all things revolve, even Jesus Christ.[3] The temple is thus portrayed as not only a place of ordinances, not only a place of binding families together, not only a place of receiving revelation—though all of this is important—but the temple is a place that first and foremost symbolically points us to Christ and the power of His infinite Atonement which is the very central power that enables us to be bound as families and to one day enter back into Father's presence.

The scriptures constantly remind us that all things given to us from God, including and especially the temple, remind us and direct us to Christ. In Moses 6:62–63, it says:

And now, behold, I say unto you: This is the plan of salvation unto all men, through the blood of mine Only Begotten, who shall come in the meridian of time.

And behold, *all things have their likeness, and all things are created and made to bear record of me*, both things which are temporal, and things which are spiritual; things which are in the heavens above, and things which are on the earth, and things which are in the earth, and things which are under the earth, both above and beneath: *all things bear record of me.* (emphasis added).

Likewise, we read in 2 Nephi 11:4 a similar admonition:

Behold, my soul delighteth in proving unto my people the truth of the coming of Christ; for, for this end hath the law of Moses been given; *and all things which have been given of God from the beginning of the world, unto man, are the typifying of him.* (emphasis added)

And finally, yet another witness of this truth:

Behold, they believed in Christ and worshiped the Father in his name, and also we worship the Father in his name. And for this intent we keep the law of Moses, *it pointing our souls to him*; and for this cause it is sanctified unto us for righteousness, even as it was accounted unto Abraham in the wilderness to be obedient unto the commands of God in offering up his son Isaac, *which is a similitude of God and his Only Begotten Son.* (Jacob 4:5; emphasis added).

Thus the temple and all its attendant teachings bear record of Christ; they typify Christ; and they point us (like the Big Dipper) to Christ. It would appear that since the beginning of the world this reminder of the centrality of Christ's Atonement has been at the heart of all that Heavenly Father endeavors to teach His children. "For behold, God knowing all things, being from everlasting to everlasting, behold, he sent angels to minister unto the children of men, to make manifest concerning the coming of Christ; and in Christ there should come every good thing" (Moroni 7:22). Adam and Eve, for example, learned this lesson vividly through the instruction of an angel in the following account given to us in the Pearl of Great Price:

And after many days an angel of the Lord appeared unto Adam, saying: Why dost thou offer sacrifices unto the Lord? And Adam said unto him: I know not, save the Lord commanded me.

And then the angel spake, saying: *This thing is a similitude of the sacrifice of the Only Begotten of the Father*, which is full of grace and truth. Wherefore, thou shalt do all that thou doest in the name of the Son, and thou shalt repent and call upon God in the name of the Son forevermore. (Moses 5:6–8; emphasis added)

The Cross of Christ as a Symbol?

There are other beautiful symbols of Christ's Atonement that we encounter in the temple. We will introduce one such symbol in a moment that is very common, yet mostly unknown or unrecognized by Latter-day Saints. However, before so doing, let us explore a preliminary concept. President Gordon B. Hinckley once taught, "This is a sanctuary of service. Most of the work done in this sacred house is performed vicariously in behalf of those who have passed beyond the veil of death. I know of no other work to compare with it. *It more nearly approaches the vicarious sacrifice of the Son of God in behalf of all mankind than any other work of which I am aware.*"[4]

Speaking of Christ's sacrifice, a question is often asked by Latter-day Saints and nonmembers alike: "If Mormons believe in Christ so much, why then is the symbol of the cross not used by the Church like many other Christian denominations?" In answer to this question, many Church members are prone to give this simple answer: "We choose to focus on Christ's life and not his death." This concise sound bite might appear convincing and rational to some, but is this the real reason we as a church choose to not use the cross as a symbol? Is it really true that we choose to not focus on Christ's death? First, let's examine a few scriptures in the Book of Mormon regarding this matter. In Jacob 1:8, we read:

> Wherefore, we would to God that we could persuade all men not to rebel against God, to provoke him to anger, but that all men would believe in Christ, *and view his death, and suffer his cross* and bear the shame of the world; wherefore, I, Jacob, take it upon me to fulfill the commandment of my brother Nephi. (emphasis added)

Also we read this statement from Mormon to his son Moroni as he summarizes the sad death and destruction that has occurred amongst the Nephite people:

> My son, be faithful in Christ; and may not the things which I have written grieve thee, to weigh thee down unto death; but may Christ lift thee up, and *may his sufferings and death*, and the showing his body unto our fathers, and his mercy and long-suffering, and the hope of his glory and of eternal life, *rest in your mind forever.* (Moroni 9:25; emphasis added)

When Christ appeared to the Nephites in the land Bountiful, the very first thing he did was to vividly instruct and remind them of his death and sufferings:

Behold, I am Jesus Christ, whom the prophets testified shall come into the world.

And behold, I am the light and the life of the world; and *I have drunk out of that bitter cup which the Father hath given me*, and have glorified the Father in *taking upon me the sins of the world*, in the which I have *suffered the will of the Father in all things* from the beginning. . . .

Arise and come forth unto me, that ye may *thrust your hands into my side, and also that ye may feel the prints of the nails in my hands and in my feet, that ye may know that I am the God of Israel, and the God of the whole earth, and have been slain for the sins of the world.* (3 Nephi 11:10–11, 14; emphasis added)

From the foregoing scriptures, we begin to challenge the notion that we as Latter-day Saints choose to not focus on Christ's death. Surely it is apparent that such a conclusion is not the case with writers of the Nephite record. Even the Savior himself dispels this mistaken notion as we have noted. Brigham Young once boldly and eloquently stated: "I would say to my young friends . . . that if you go on a mission to preach the gospel with lightness and frivolity in your hearts . . . and not having your minds riveted—yes, I may say riveted—on the cross of Christ, you will go and return in vain. . . . Let your minds be centered on your missions, and labor earnestly to bring souls to Christ."[5] President Hinckley likewise reminds us of our absolute need to remember the savior's sufferings and death:

No member of this Church must ever forget the terrible price paid by our Redeemer, who gave His life that all men might live—the agony of Gethsemane, the bitter mockery of His trial, the vicious crown of thorns tearing at His flesh, the blood cry of the mob before Pilate, the lonely burden of His heavy walk along the way to Calvary, the terrifying pain as great nails pierced His hands and feet, the fevered torture of His body as He hung that tragic day. . . . *We cannot forget that. We must never forget it*, for here our Savior, our Redeemer, the Son of God, gave Himself, a vicarious sacrifice for each of us.[6]

Another witness of this reality can be found in a simple perusal of many of our sacred sacrament hymns, which lead us to the realization that we not only focus on Christ, but we very much focus and remember his sufferings, crucifixion, and death. Indeed, this worshipful remembrance of Christ's Atonement and death is the central focus of the ordinance of the sacrament, the focus being on the emblems of his flesh and blood which was shed for us (see D&C 20:77–79). In fact, all ordinances of the restored gospel serve a similar purpose. Elder Jeffrey R. Holland reminded the Saints of this fact when he clearly stated: *"Every ordinance of the gospel focuses in one way or another on the atonement of the Lord Jesus Christ,* and surely that is why this particular ordinance [the sacrament] with all its symbolism and imagery comes to us more readily and more repeatedly than any other in our life."[7]

Consider the ordinance of baptism in light of all of this. When asked what baptism symbolizes, some Church members quickly respond that this is a symbol of having our sins "washed" away. This is true in part, but to leave it at that avoids the real meaning. In the Doctrine and Covenants, we discover a truer, deeper meaning as to the meaning of the symbolism of the baptismal ordinance:

> Herein is glory and honor, and immortality and eternal life—*The ordinance of baptism by water, to be immersed therein in order to answer to the likeness of the dead,* that one principle might accord with the other; to be *immersed in the water and come forth out of the water is in the likeness of the resurrection of the dead in coming forth out of their graves. . . .*
>
> Consequently, the baptismal font was instituted *as a similitude of the grave,* and was commanded to be in a place underneath where the living are wont to assemble, to show forth the living and the dead, and *that all things may have their likeness,* and that they may accord one with another—that which is earthly conforming to that which is heavenly. (D&C 128:12–13; emphasis added)

Paul said it this way in his epistle to the Romans:

> Therefore *we are buried with him by baptism into death*: that like as Christ was raised up from the dead by the glory of the Father, even so we also should walk in newness of life.
>
> For if we have been planted together in the likeness of his death, *we shall be also in the likeness of his resurrection.* (Romans 6:4–5; emphasis added)

This is to say that baptism is first and foremost a reminder of Christ's death and burial, and, a reminder of His resurrection and ours! Once again, as Elder Holland stated, all ordinances remind us, in one way or another, not only of Christ's Atonement, but of His death as well. Even the ordinances of the endowment and temple marriage sealing ceremony focus not only on Christ, but symbolically remind us how He suffered and died. This might sound strange to some, but the saving ordinances of the gospel are "death" ceremonies—but with this provision in them: from death (Christ's death) there comes life, even eternal life. This model is part of and can be seen in each of the saving ordinances of the restored gospel.

So why then do we not use the cross as a symbol in our Church? Noted Latter-day Saint scholar Robert L. Millet once offered the following explanation:

> We have no quarrel with those who speak reverently of the cross, for so did those whose writings compose a significant portion of the New Testament and those who spoke or wrote what is contained in our own scriptural records. The cross is a symbol. We are not opposed to symbols, for our people erect statues of the angel Moroni atop our most sacred edifices and wear CTR rings on their hand. On a number of occasions when I have been asked why the Latter-day Saints do not believe in the saving efficacy of the cross, and when I have corrected the false impression by referring to [latter-day scripture], a follow-up question comes: "Well then, if you people really do claim to be Christian, why do you not have crosses on your buildings, your vestments, or your literature?" After consulting with a few LDS cultural historians, it appears that crosses were seldom if ever placed on our meetinghouses. Inasmuch as many of our early converts came from a Puritan background, they, like the Puritans, were essentially anti-ceremonial, including the non-use of crosses. For that matter, early Baptists did not have crosses on their churches for a long time, at least until they began to move into mainstream Protestantism.[8]

In short, we as a Church just never adopted it as a symbol; many other non-Catholic Christian churches eventually did. Originally, it was the exclusive symbol of Catholicism, and even they didn't use it in the first few Christian centuries since the cross was not considered a virtuous or admirable symbol. No, even before it became a symbol of Christianity, it was a terrifying reminder of what Jesus and many thousands of others had ignominiously suffered. Some scholars report that the cross did not appear in churches as a symbol of veneration until AD 431 and crosses on steeples did not appear until 586. It was not until the sixth century that crucifixes were sanctioned by the Roman church.[9]

The Temple and the Circle and the Square

Although we do not adorn our church buildings with the crucifix, that is not to say that we do not love, remember, or venerate Christ's sufferings and death. Likewise, the absence of this icon is not to say that we do not have a symbol, which serves as a reminder for us as to the importance of the Atonement of Christ, for we do! Although most members may have never recognized it, there is a simple, basic architectural design that can be seen in and on, not all, but most of our temples. The symbol is that of a circle framed by a square.

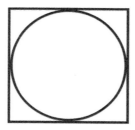

Before discussing some historical considerations and potential meanings, let us first see and recognize the frequent use of those symbols on many of our temples and church buildings:

Spokane Washington Temple

Bountiful Utah Temple fence

Las Vegas Nevada Temple

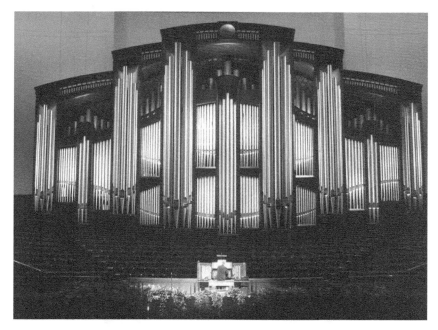

Pipe Organ at the LDS Conference Center—circle and square at top

Mount Timpanogos Utah Temple front doors

Salt Lake City Temple front doors

Spokane Washington Temple windows

What then is the meaning of the symbol of the circle and square? First of all it is a beautiful and yet simple symbol that is a powerful reminder not only of the purpose of temples but of the main focus of the temple—Jesus Christ and His infinite Atonement. The square was anciently a symbol for the earth. Some might even recognize the literary phrase, "the four corners of the earth." This is not referring to four geographical corners on the earth, but to the symbol of the earth. Why a square? Well, the lines on a square have definite beginning and ending points, just like this mortal probation—birth, death, health, sickness, sunrise, sunset, etc.—whereas the circle is the ancient symbol for the heavens. In the circle we see that which does not end, eternity—God's course is one eternal round, etc.

So, what is it that we are to gather from the circle and the square being brought together in one, especially as we find these symbols so amply displayed on many of our temples? Simply put, the temple, like the circle and square, is a place where heaven and earth come together in one. This oneness is only possible because of Christ's Atonement, which when broken down into its constituent parts literally means the "at-one-ment"! Thus, the temple is a place of covenant between imperfect mortal man, and a perfect omniscient, omnipotent Heavenly Father. It is a place where we are reminded in powerful and prolific ways that salvation is only in and through the Atonement of Jesus Christ.

One further thought is worth mentioning. Anciently, if one wanted to make a circle, a compass would be used; if one desired to make a square that was plum, the instrument to be used was a builder's square. The compass and the square are the tools one uses to make the completed design of the circle and square. It is interesting to note that the first Nauvoo Temple  had a weather vane with a flying angel on top with the symbol of the compass and square directly above.[10] Faithful endowed members will realize and appreciate the fact that, symbolically, they are given as a gift (or endowment) the tools necessary (compass and the square) to make an at-one-ment in their lives (the completed design of the circle and the square).

With regards to the compass and the square, one scholar has noted that temple garments "bear several simple marks of orientation toward the gospel principles of obedience, truth, life, and discipleship in Christ."[11]

Thus, the circle and the square—which are displayed abundantly on many LDS temples with their corresponding tools of the compass and square—that we symbolically take out of the temple with us can serve as powerful reminders not only of sacred covenants made in the temple, but also of the power by which those covenants are made efficacious— even the power of the Atonement of Jesus Christ. Elder David A. Bednar taught, "The temple is a point of intersection between heaven and earth. In this sacred place, holy work will be performed through selfless service and love. The temple reminds me of all that is good and beautiful in the world."[12] Truly, the temple is wholly and completely a beautiful symbol of Christ and His infinite Atonement.[13]

Notes

1. Russell M. Nelson, "Personal Preparation for Temple Blessings," *Ensign*, May 2001, 32.
2. Boyd K. Packer, "The Mediator," *Ensign*, May 1977, 56.
3. See Hugh Nibley, *Temple and Cosmos: Beyond the Ignorant Present* (Salt Lake City: Deseret Book, 1992); see also James E. Talmage, *The House of the Lord* (Salt Lake City: Deseret Book, 1912), 178.
4. Gordon B. Hinckley, "The Salt Lake Temple," *Ensign*, March 1993, 5; emphasis added.
5. Brigham Young, in *Journal of Discourses* 12:33–34.
6. Gordon B. Hinckley, "The Symbol of Our Faith," *Ensign*, April 2005, 4; emphasis added.
7. Jeffery R. Holland, "'This Do in Remembrance of Me,'" *Ensign*, November 1995, 67; emphasis added.
8. Robert L. Millet, "Jesus Christ and Salvation," in *No Weapon Shall Prosper: A Response to Anti-Mormon Views*, ed. Robert L. Millet (Provo, UT: Religious Studies Center, Brigham Young University, 2011), 329–344.
9. See Robert L. Millet, *What Happened to the Cross?: Distinctive LDS Teachings* (Salt Lake City: Deseret Book, 2007).

10. Matthew B. Brown and Paul Thomas Smith, *Symbols in Stone: Symbolism on the Early Temples of the Restoration* (Salt Lake City: Covenant Communications, 1997), 105.

11. Evelyn T. Marshall, "Garments," in *Encyclopedia of Mormonism*, ed. Daniel H. Ludlow 5 vols. (1992), 2:534.

12. David A. Bednar's Facebook page, August 25, 2014, accessed May 9, 2017, https://www.facebook.com/lds.david.a.bednar.

13. For a further exposition on the history and use of the ancient symbol of the Circle and Square, see Hugh Nibley, *Temple and Cosmos: Beyond the Ignorant Present* (Salt Lake City: Deseret Book, 1992).

Two

The Temple and the Four Pillars of Eternity

My soul delighteth in proving unto my people that save Christ should come all men must perish. For if there be no Christ there be no God; and if there be no God we are not, for there could have been no creation. But there is a God.
(2 Nephi 11:6–7)

Many years ago, I was teaching a family home evening lesson, and the topic was centered on the characteristics of our Heavenly Father. The lesson was not only basic in content but simple in delivery as well. My oldest daughter, who was about nine years old at the time, raised her hand to ask a question. "Dad, where did Heavenly Father come from?"

I responded that Heavenly Father was an exalted man and that He was once like us, meaning that He was mortal and lived on an earth like ours. I quoted off the top of my head the couplet from Lorenzo Snow that so many Latter-day Saints are fond of referencing: "As man is, God once was, and as God is, man may be."

She was speechless, stunned, and thrilled at the same time. Then came her next question: "Dad, does that mean that Heavenly Father had a Heavenly Father?!" I replied in the affirmative. "Wait! Dad! Who then was Heavenly Father's Heavenly Father's Heavenly Father? Whoa . . . DAD, wait . . . who was the first Heavenly Father?!" Her mind was ready to burst. It would have been a hilarious moment had it not been such a sincere, poignant, and in-depth moment at the same time. We had just run into that philosophical wall that youth and adults often run into when exploring such questions.

In the hymn "If You Could Hie to Kolob," it begs answer to the question in the first verse: Can you "find out the generation where Gods began to be?" The implied answer in the verses that follow give the baffling, mind numbing, and incomprehensible answer: "There is no end . . ." No end, nor is there a beginning to the cycles of exaltation that have been occurring throughout eternity.

Although I quickly ran out of answers with my daughter that night, we ended up having an incredible discussion about some of the fundamental realities of our existence and at the same time explored some of the core doctrines relating to God's plan of salvation. I like to refer to these doctrines as the Four Pillars of Eternity. These doctrines, interestingly, are not only the four core doctrines of God's plan, but are also the four foundational doctrines of the temple endowment. The endowment is thus a school that teaches us not only about *our* existence, but the very nature *of* existence and the reality that comprises all of our lives.

Pillars of Eternity

The term *pillars of eternity* is not new. Others have used this term before but usually in the context of just three pillars. Elder Bruce R. McConkie has stated: "The three pillars of eternity [are] the three great eternal verities upon which salvation rests." Further he states that these are "the three greatest events that have ever occurred in all eternity . . . the three events, preeminent and transcendent above all others, [which] are the creation, the fall, and the atonement."[1]

Similarly, Elder Nelson of the Quorum of the Twelve has said: "As it is central to the plan, we should try to comprehend the meaning of the Atonement. Before we can comprehend it, though, we must understand the fall of Adam. And before we can fully appreciate the Fall, we must first comprehend the Creation. These three events—the Creation, the Fall, and the Atonement—are three preeminent pillars of God's plan, and they are doctrinally interrelated."[2]

Not to upstage any of these aforementioned voices, I would propose the addition of a "fourth" pillar of eternity—namely, exaltation or Godhood (eternal life would be another synonym). The following chart shows the interrelationship that occurs between these doctrines:

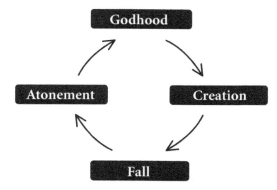

This fourth pillar is not only worth mentioning but warrants inclusion with the three pillars because it is the end outcome and desired goal and purpose of the plan of salvation, not to mention some modern prophets have suggested such.[3] Without eternal life and exaltation (i.e., Godhood) there could be no creation and thus continuance of this eternal cycle. Indeed, Elder McConkie claims:

> Without any one of them all things would lose their purpose and meaning, and the plans and designs of Deity would come to naught.
>
> If there had been no creation, we would not be, neither the earth, nor any form of life upon its face. All things, all the primal elements, would be without form and void. God would have no spirit children; there would be no mortal probation; and none of us would be on the way to *immortality and eternal life.*[4]

Similarly, Elder Boyd K. Packer has stated: "This we know! This simple truth! Had there been no Creation, no Fall, there should have been no need for any Atonement, neither a Redeemer to mediate for us. Then Christ need not have been."[5] In short, God creates things; He sets up conditions whereby things can fall;[6] He provides a way so those things can be redeemed through the Atonement; and all of this so that we can become exalted beings one day like our Father and Mother in heaven—even gods and goddesses. And what do gods do? They create things—and the cycle continues.

This reality is encapsulated so well in the following verses from the Book of Mormon: "My soul delighteth in proving unto my people that save Christ should come all men must perish. For if there be no Christ there be no God; and if there be no God we are not, for there could have been no creation. But there is a God" (2 Nephi 11:6–7).

Another way to say this is if there be no Atonement (no Christ), then there can be no gods; and if there are no gods, then things cannot be created. We then are doing (and going through) the same thing that our Heavenly Father went through and that which His Heavenly father went through. This pedagogical pattern of revelatory repetition is central to the theology of the temple. In summary, we are following a grand, eternal template, as suggested by Orson Pratt:

> The dealing of God towards his children from the time they are first born in Heaven, through all their successive stages of existence, until they are redeemed, perfected, and made Gods, is a pattern after which all other worlds are dealt with. . . . The creation, fall, and redemption of all future worlds with their inhabitants will be conducted upon the same general plan. . . . The Father of our spirits has only been doing that which His progenitors did before Him. Each succeeding generation of Gods follow the example of the preceding ones. . . . [The same plan of redemption is carried out] by which more ancient worlds have been redeemed. . . . Thus will worlds and systems of worlds . . . be multiplied in endless succession through the infinite depths of boundless space; some telestial, some terrestrial, and some celestial, differing in their glory.[7]

The diagram below is thus an illustration of this reality, and, an amplification of the previous chart in extended version:

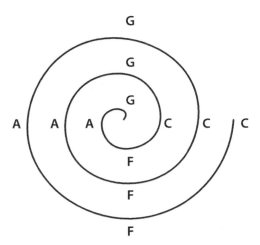

In the holy temple, all teaching centers on and derives itself from these four foundational doctrines. Furthermore, we learn therein that this cycle, which produces exaltation and eternal lives (see D&C 132), is an unending cycle throughout all eternity. No wonder that in the ordinance of the endowment, the longest time wise of all the saving ordinances, we find each one of these doctrines amply taught not only in their beautiful, allegorical fulness but also taught in an interconnected fashion with the other core doctrines. It is interesting to note that prophets from the Book of Mormon taught these very same doctrines as well to their listeners:

> And it came to pass that when Aaron saw that the king would believe his words, he began from the *creation* of Adam, reading the scriptures unto the king—how *God created man* after his own image, and that God gave him commandments, and that because of transgression, *man had fallen.*
>
> And Aaron did expound unto him the scriptures from the creation of Adam, laying *the fall of man* before him, and their carnal state *and also the plan of redemption*, which was prepared from the foundation of the world, *through Christ*, for all whosoever would believe on his name. . . .
>
> And it came to pass that after Aaron had expounded these things unto him, the king said: What shall I do that I may have *this eternal life* of which thou hast spoken? (Alma 22:12–13, 15; emphasis added)

The Fourth Pillar: Exaltation, Eternal Life, and Godhood

In the next few chapters of this book, we will explore in greater detail the first three of these doctrinal pillars of eternity. Before so doing it would be helpful to say a few words about this fourth pillar, namely, exaltation, eternal life, or godhood. All of these aforementioned terms are actually synonyms. Other scriptural terms describe this exalted state as well. Those who become exalted, who inherit eternal life, are individuals who also receive "eternal increase" (D&C 131); they receive "all power" and the "continuation of the seeds" (D&C 132:19–20); they receive the "father's kingdom" and "all that the Father hath" (D&C 84:33–38); they are filled "with His glory" and are "made equal with Him" (D&C 88:107); they become "joint heirs" with Christ (Romans 8:17) and they "sit in [His] throne" (Revelation 3:21). In short, they become gods and goddesses. Although some might consider such status as blasphemous or downright impossible, we learn from the Savior Himself that such an attainment is not only possible, but it is likewise commanded. "Be ye therefore perfect, even as your Father which is in heaven is perfect" (Matthew 5:48). C. S. Lewis's words are memorable:

> Imagine yourself as a living house. God comes in to rebuild that house. At first, perhaps, you can understand what He is doing. He is getting the drains right and stopping the leaks in the roof and so on: you knew that those jobs needed doing and so you are not surprised. But presently He starts knocking the house about in a way that hurts abominably and does not seem to make sense. What on earth is He up to? The explanation is that He is building quite a different house from the one you thought of—throwing out a new wing here, putting on an extra floor there, running up towers, making courtyards. You thought you were going to be made into a decent little cottage: but He is building a palace. . . .
>
> The command "Be ye perfect" is not idealistic gas. Nor is it a command to do the impossible. He is going to make us into creatures that can obey that command. He said (in the Bible) that we were 'gods' and He is going to make good His words. If we let Him—for we can prevent Him, if we choose—He will make the feeblest and filthiest of us into a god or goddess, dazzling, radiant, immortal creature, pulsating all through with such energy and joy and wisdom and love as we cannot now imagine. . . . *The process will be long and in parts very painful; but that is what we are in for.* Nothing less. He meant what He said.[8]

Lewis's words remind us that such a lofty achievement, while certainly possible, is not something that will occur immediately. The First Presidency once taught: "Man is the child of God, formed in the divine image and endowed with divine attributes, and even as the infant son of an earthly father and mother is capable in due time of becoming a man, so the undeveloped offspring of celestial parentage is capable, by experience through ages and aeons, of evolving into a God."[9]

The Default Position of Salvation and Exaltation

The preceding analogy from the first presidency is intriguing and is worth a closer examination. The question is not whether the infant will develop into a full grown adult or not—that has already been determined. The child is genetically engineered to become such. We are preprogrammed, if you will, to achieve our biological destiny. It was foreordained long ago. No amount of wishing, worrying, trying, or not trying will change things.

Similarly, we all, being sons and daughters of heavenly parents, are engineered and designed from the beginning to become exalted beings one day. In fact, we have been given exaltation provisionally. The question is not whether we will earn it, but whether or not we will let go of what we already have. We have the promises; we have the assurance. The default position of salvation and exaltation is not that we don't have it and are trying to get to it, but that we already have it and we are here on earth trying to decide if we will finish becoming what we were designed to be. Eternal life isn't a door prize or salary payment—it is a realization or attainment of our divine and eternal potential.

Moses realized this truth when he declared to the Lord: "Thou hast made me, and *given unto me a right to thy throne*, and not of myself, *but through thine own grace*" (Moses 7:59; emphasis added). What a beautiful truth. We have *a right* to the throne! This is to say, we have a right to exaltation and eternal life. It is indeed our birthright—this is what we were divinely engineered to become!

The issue then is not whether we are ever going to do enough to "earn" eternal life; that has already been done by the Savior—through His "own grace" as the scripture says. No, the issue is whether or not we will let go of what we already have.

Similarly, in Abraham 3:26 we read: "And they who *keep their first estate* shall be added upon; and they who *keep not their first estate* shall not have glory in the same kingdom with those who *keep their first estate*; and they who *keep their second estate* shall have glory added upon their heads for ever and ever" (emphasis added). We do not "earn" our estates, we keep them. In 2 Nephi 2:4, we are told that "the way is prepared from the fall of man, and salvation is free." Salvation in any form (not just physical death) is not something we earn—it has already been given to us. The only issue to decide is if we will hold on to this precious gift and endowment. Such a realization should fill our hearts and minds with unrestrained peace and serenity. It should cause us to worry less and rejoice more and more. The Lord's teachings on this matter are consistent and sure:

Fear not, and be just, for *the Kingdom is ours*.[10]

I will be merciful unto you, for *I have given unto you the kingdom*. (D&C 64:4; emphasis added)

For *ye are lawful heirs*, according to the flesh, and have been hid from the world with Christ in God. (D&C 86:9; emphasis added)

Peace be with you; my blessings continue with you. *For even yet the kingdom is yours, and shall be forever, if you fall not* from your steadfastness. (D&C 82:23–24; emphasis added)

And ye cannot bear all things now; nevertheless, be of good cheer, for I will lead you along. *The kingdom is yours and the blessings thereof are yours, and the riches of eternity are yours.* (D&C 78:18; emphasis added)

And if ye be Christ's, then are ye Abraham's seed, *and heirs according to the promise.* (Galatians 3:29; emphasis added; cf. Romans 9:6–7)

To him that overcometh *will I grant to sit with me in my throne*, even as I also overcame, and am set down with my Father in his throne. (Revelation 3:21; emphasis added)

In Matthew 5:5, we learn that the meek do not earn the earth, they "inherit the earth" (see also Alma 5:51; 3 Nephi 11:38; Alma 5:58; Alma 40:26). Many people do not have to do anything to receive an inheritance apart from being born into a family with riches—and we have *all* been born into an eternal family with eternal riches. In Mosiah 27: 25–26 it says: "And the Lord said unto me: Marvel not that all mankind, yea, men and women, all nations, kindreds, tongues and people, must be born again; yea, born of God, changed from their carnal and fallen state, to a state of righteousness, being redeemed of God, becoming his sons and daughters; and thus they become new creatures; and unless they do this, they can in nowise *inherit the kingdom of God*" (emphasis added). True it is that when we inherit something it isn't earned—it is a free gift given; however, even though we don't earn an inheritance, we can, if we are not careful, disinherit ourselves through disobedience and unrepented sins.

With the knowledge that the "promises are yours" (D&C 132:31) we should quit worrying and start living and becoming. They key is to never give up trying . . . because we will get there. The Lord said to Oliver Granger: "Therefore, let him contend earnestly for the redemption of the First Presidency of my Church, saith the Lord; *and when he falls he shall rise again*, for his sacrifice shall be more sacred unto me than his increase, saith the Lord" (D&C 117:13; emphasis added). President Boyd K. Packer's commentary on this verse is memorable:

Some worry endlessly over missions that were missed, or marriages that did not turn out, or babies that did not arrive, or children that seem lost, or dreams unfulfilled, or because age limits what they can do. I do not think it pleases the Lord when we worry because we think we never do enough or that what we do is never good enough.

Some needlessly carry a heavy burden of guilt which could be removed through confession and repentance.

The Lord did not say of Oliver, "[If] he falls," but "When he falls he shall rise again."[11]

We all make mistakes. We all "fall short of the glory of God" (Romans 3:23). The key is to never give up, to keep rising, because eventually we will get to our eternal destiny if we do not quit. C. S. Lewis has said:

We may, indeed, be sure that perfect chastity—like perfect charity—will not be attained by any merely human efforts. You must ask for God's help. Even when you have done so, it may seem to you for a long time that no help, or less help than you need, is being given. Never mind. After each failure, ask forgiveness, pick yourself up, and try again. Very often what God first helps us towards is not the virtue itself but just this power of always trying again. For however important chastity (or courage, or truthfulness, or any other virtue) may be, this process trains us in habits of the soul which are more important still. It cures our illusions about ourselves and teaches us to depend on God. We learn, on the one hand, that we cannot trust ourselves even in our best moments, and, on the other, that we need not despair even in our worst, for our failures are forgiven. The only fatal thing is to sit down content with anything less than perfection.[12]

Conclusion

The temple is a saintly school that teaches us clearly and consistently about the four pillars of eternity—the four grand and central doctrines that undergird our eternal destiny. We receive the promises of eternal life and exaltation in the temple—these are blessings not earned nor merited. No, they are received! "For what doth it profit a man if a gift is bestowed upon him, and he receive not the gift? Behold, he rejoices not in that which is given unto him, neither rejoices in him who is the giver of the gift" (D&C 88:33). We go to the temple not to "earn" power from on high, but to be "endowed with power from on high" (see D&C 38:32, 38; 95:8; 105:11).

Elder David B. Haight once said: "A temple is a place in which those whom He has chosen are endowed with power from on high—*a power which enables us to use our gifts and capabilities*—with greater intelligence and increased effectiveness in order to bring to pass our Heavenly Father's purposes in our own lives and the lives of those we love."[13] Our choice is to decide what to do with that enabling power so freely given. We should never worry, for we have the promises. President Monson once counseled: "As a result of the sacred ordinances performed in the holy house of God, no light need be permanently extinguished, no voice permanently stilled, no place in our heart permanently left vacant."[14]

Notes

1. Bruce R. McConkie, "The Three Pillars of Eternity" (Brigham Young University devotional, February 17, 1981), 1, speeches.byu.edu.
2. Russell M. Nelson, "Constancy amid Change," *Ensign*, November 1993, 33.
3. Elder D. Todd Christofferson alludes to these four pillars in "Why Marriage, Why Family," *Ensign*, May 2015.
4. Bruce R. McConkie, "The Three Pillars of Eternity" (Brigham Young University devotional, February 17, 1981), 1, speeches.byu.edu; emphasis added.
5. Boyd K. Packer, "Atonement, Agency, Accountability," *Ensign*, May 1988.
6. God cannot create fallen things, he can only set up conditions whereby things can fall through the exercise of agency. Things must become fallen as an eternal principle, since there "must needs be opposition in all things!"
7. Orson Pratt, "The Pre-existence of Man," *The Seer*, September 1853, 134–35.
8. C. S. Lewis, *Mere Christianity*, rev. ed. (1952; repr., New York: HarperOne, 2015), 206; emphasis added.
9. "The Origin of Man, by the First Presidency of the Church," *Improvement Era,* November 1909, 75.
10. "Redeemer of Israel," *Hymns*, no. 6; emphasis added.
11. Boyd K. Packer, "The Least of These," *Ensign*, November 2004.
12. C. S. Lewis, *Mere Christianity*, rev. ed. (1952; repr., New York: HarperOne, 2015), 102.
13. David B. Haight, "Come to the House of the Lord," *Ensign*, May 1992, 15.
14. Thomas S. Monson, *Be Your Best Self* (Salt Lake City: Deseret Book, 1979), 54.

Three

The Temple and
the Creation

One of the most integral and interesting aspects of LDS temple worship is found in the ordinance of the endowment. This extensive ceremony comprises many elements of truth, commitments, teachings, warnings, covenants, and instruction—all of which teach the things of eternity. President Gordon B. Hinckley once said that the temple, and by implication the endowment, "becomes a school of instruction in the sweet and sacred things of God. Here we have outlined the plan of a loving Father in behalf of His sons and daughters of all generations. Here we have sketched before us the odyssey of man's eternal journey from premortal existence through this life to the life beyond. Great fundamental and basic truths are taught with clarity and simplicity well within the understanding of all who hear."[1] One of these basic truths that are taught in the endowment is the account of the creation of all things: the earth, plants and animals, and most notably—mankind. In this chapter ,we look at the doctrine of the creation and how it fits into temple worship as well as the symbolic implications that this doctrine has with the Atonement of Jesus Christ.

Disclaimers about the Creation

Before proceeding though, it should be understood that there are some things we know and some things we don't know about the creation, especially as it relates to the creation of man. The following will be given as disclaimers so as to place our discussion about these matters in proper doctrinal context.[2]

Disclaimer 1: Our understanding about the Creation is limited.

There are some things we simply do not know and do not understand with regards to the creation accounts as seen in scripture and as portrayed in the temple endowment ceremony. Not everything has been revealed on this matter. Speaking of this very issue, Elder Bruce R. McConkie once said:

> Our analysis properly begins with the frank recital that *our knowledge about the Creation is limited.* We do not know the how and why and when of all things. Our finite limitations are such that we could not comprehend them if they were revealed to us in all their glory, fullness, and perfection. *What has been revealed is that portion of the Lord's eternal word which we must believe and understand if we are to envision the truth about the Fall and the Atonement* and thus become heirs of salvation. This is all we are obligated to know in our day.[3]

It is interesting to note in this statement that Heavenly Father has given us enough about the Creation to help us understand the truth about the Atonement. The importance of this concept cannot be understated. In essence, we fail as teachers when we try to use the revealed account of the Creation to teach about creationism! The purpose of the Creation accounts in the scriptures (of which there are three) is not to teach us about the Creation. The purpose of these accounts is to actually teach us about the Atonement of Jesus Christ. Elder Neal A. Maxwell once observed: "The Creator of the Universe *does not choose to dazzle his audiences with data concerning the Creation.* Rather, as a Perfect and Loving Shepherd, he is interested in the central needs and concerns of his sheep in his many folds."[4]

One example of our understanding being limited can be found in a discussion on the "days of creation." We are told in the scriptural and temple accounts that the earth was created in six days. A lot of people over the ages and even in the Church have speculated what the term "day" means. It is important to consider the doctrines of God's time relative to the Fall of Adam when discussing the doctrine of the Creation. In 2 Nephi 2:21, we learn that because of Adam's transgression his "time was lengthened," perhaps suggesting that linear time as we know it did not exist before the Fall. This notion is strengthened in Abraham 5:13: "But of the tree of knowledge of good and evil, thou shalt not eat of it; for *in the time* that thou eatest thereof, thou shalt surely die. Now I, Abraham, saw that *it was after the Lord's time*, which was after the time of Kolob; *for as yet the Gods had not appointed unto Adam his reckoning*" (emphasis added). These scriptures both suggest that mortal time as we know it not only commenced with the Fall of Adam but that conditions in the Garden of Eden (and during the periods of Creation) were "after the Lord's time," where past, present, and future are all one (see D&C 130:6–8). Although it's hard for us to wrap our minds around that actual concept, when we consider its ramifications, there are new perspectives that can be given to the process of Creation.

Often teachers and students of the gospel debate about the "length of time" of the days of Creation. A biblical literalist would claim it took six days, meaning of course, six twenty-four-hour time periods. Some Latter-day Saints argue another approach, claiming that it took six thousand years, since each day for God is a thousand years on earth.[5] Some individuals use the book of Abraham (see chapter 4) to argue even another point of view that there were six indefinite time periods all called "days," concluding that a "day" of Creation could be millions of years or more. Students who lean toward the theory of evolution rather than toward creationism often find this third approach appealing.

However, if the Creation occurred before mortal time (as we know it) was instituted, none of these approaches has merit. Why? Because all deal in one way or another with linear time. When we consider that the Creation occurred in God's time, we realize that evolutionary claims of science, along with discussions of dinosaurs, plate tectonics, million-year ages and epochs, etc., need not dissuade us from believing in the Creation account. Nor do we need to feel any unjustified, dogmatic allegiance to our interpretation of the Creation and thus be dismissive of evolutionary claims. We need not worry. Though we do not understand all concerning the Creation, nor will we until the Second Coming (see D&C 101:32–34), the idea of *God's time* being in play before the Fall opens up a myriad of possibilities. Perhaps the term *days* is used in the Creation accounts as a device given by God to man so that he might form some sort of rudimentary metric by which to envision the complexities of those things that are unexplainable because of the timeless dimension in which God resides.

Doctrine and Covenants 29:31–32 explains: "For by the power of my Spirit created I them; yea, all things both spiritual and temporal— First spiritual, secondly temporal, which is the *beginning* of my work; and again, first temporal, and secondly spiritual, which is the *last* of my work" (emphasis added). From these verses, we learn the simple truth that all things are first created spiritually, then temporally (or physically). This is precisely what we are taught in Moses 3:5, wherein the Lord states: "For I, the Lord God, created all things, of which I have spoken, spiritually, before they were naturally upon the face of the earth."

However, according to Doctrine and Covenants 29, this process is just the "beginning" of God's creative work. Verse 32 clarifies that God takes those "temporal," or physical, creations and creates them spiritually again. This is described as being the "last" of God's work. This does not mean that all things created, including mankind, will ultimately end up as spirits again. There is a difference between "being a spirit" and "being a spiritual being." To become a spiritual being is the process of coming to earth, where our spirits are first clothed in an earthly or physical body and then undergo the process of being "born again," as Christ taught Nicodemus, "by water and the spirit" thus putting off the natural man.[6]

Now that we think we are beginning to understand things a bit, we read D&C 29:33: "Speaking unto you *that you may naturally understand*; but unto myself *my works have no end*, neither beginning; but it is given unto you that ye may understand, because ye have asked it of me and are agreed" (emphasis added). It is as though the carpet has been pulled out from under us! After describing to us the full process of Creation, the Lord says: "Actually, that's not quite how it happened. I'm just giving you a basic framework of principles you can understand in the time-bound realm in which you live. Actually, there is no beginning or end to the creative work." We stand all amazed. He simply asks us to study and pray, to have the faith to accept things as they are, to realize that "[His] ways are higher than [ours]" (see Isaiah 55:9), and to "believe in [Him]; believe that he is, and that he created all things, both in heaven and in earth; believe that he has all wisdom, and all power, both in heaven and in earth; believe that man doth not comprehend all the things which the Lord can comprehend" (Mosiah 4:9).

Once again, we need not worry about dinosaurs, plate tectonics, Neanderthals, and other such things. We simply do not know how everything worked in a sequence. Some people likewise get perplexed because there is a different sequence of the days of Creation in Genesis than there is in the book of Moses or the book of Abraham or in the temple. Which account correct? It does not matter. It is just verbiage that Heavenly Father gives us to have a beginning place with which to start our understanding.

As Church members receive their endowment and participate in this beautiful ceremony repeatedly throughout their lives, they should take care not to construe every single aspect of the Creation account as being exactly literal. There are only basics given, which as we have said before, serve the purpose of helping us not so much to understand the exact specifics of the Creation, but rather, to understand that which Father in Heaven is teaching us about Christ's Atonement.

Disclaimer 2: We have a duty to accept what has been revealed.

True it is that there are many things that have not been revealed with the Creation; however, the Lord has revealed some truths about it, and we should do our best to understand what those truths are. At Brigham Young University, there is a student newspaper called the *Daily Universe*. About once a year, when I was an undergraduate student there in the 1990s, this weird thing would happen. Someone would write a letter to the editor. They would always couch it in a very sophisticated tone, and it would be something like this, "You know, the Church never has revealed an official position on evolution and the origin of man." A couple days later, a creationist student would write in, "You heathenous, blasphemous, R-rated-movie-watching student, you!" or something like that. Then attacks would be launched from all sides. The issue would die down after two or three weeks, and then nine or ten months later, it would rear its ugly head again. I saw that debate rage four or five times while I was a student at BYU.

Now, a question to consider: does the Church have an official position on evolution? In a statement from the BYU board of trustees printed in a packet for BYU students in 1992, we read the following: "Although there has never been a formal declaration from the first presidency addressing the general matter of organic evolution as a process for the development of biological species, plants, animals, phylums, these documents make clear the official position of the church regarding the origin of man."[7] So, does the Church have an official position about evolution? No. However, they do have an official position about the origin of man.

Although these questions sound similar, there is a big difference as to their answer and implication. The Church does not comment on evolution. The Church's official position regarding the origin of man can be found and summarized in an official statement from a 1909 declaration called "The Origin of Man." We will reference this document later in this chapter as we discuss the true origin of Adam and Eve.

Disclaimer 3: More regarding the Creation will be revealed at the Second Coming.

In Doctrine and Covenants 101:32–34 it says, "Yea, verily I say unto you, in that day when the Lord shall come, *He shall reveal all things*—Things which have passed, and hidden things which no man knew, *things of the earth, by which it was made*, and the purpose and the end thereof—Things most precious, things that are above, and things that are beneath, things that are in the earth, and upon the earth, and in heaven" (emphasis added).

While pursuing a doctoral degree in sociology of religion at Purdue University, I had the opportunity to study the theory of evolution quite deeply. There was a professor in the anthropology department who happened to be a good friend of mine. He was not only a Latter-day Saint but also a local branch president. One semester, I discovered he was teaching a class in organic evolution. I went up to him one day and chided him: "What do you think of the irony of that? Here you are, an LDS branch president, teaching organic evolution at a secular university!"

I was only trying to tease him, but he said something really profound. He said, "You have got to understand something. As an anthropologist, as a scientist, I do not believe in theories. As a scientist, I *use* theories." Do you see the difference? A good scientist does not believe in a theory, a good scientist uses a theory. A theory is the best that empirical knowledge has produced. It is the current, in-vogue, cutting-edge way of looking at things. Such theories are also subject to change. I was impressed and instructed by what my friend shared.

I was watching a documentary many years ago, and it featured a world-leading anthropologist from a prestigious university. The moderator doing the interview was asking this scholar a series of questions. At one point, as they were talking about all the missing gaps in the evolutionary chain, the moderator said, "So what you're telling me is there's a lot of missing gaps." This anthropologist said, "Oh yeah, there's a lot." Then the moderator said, "But we are filling them in pretty quickly." The anthropologist replied, "Well yeah, we are filling them in and we are coming across a lot of knowledge pretty quickly these days, but at the rate we are filling them in we won't be able to fill in all the missing gaps for over a million years."

Some things we will not know until the Second Coming. It is my opinion that Latter-days Saints should be encouraged to pursue learning in the scientific fields. Let's learn all we can and not be afraid of knowledge.

Disclaimer 4: We always need to strive to find a balance between science and religion.

There is no need for contention, especially in the Church of Jesus Christ of Latter-day Saints. There is no need to belittle one who tends to be more of a creationist, nor is there need to belittle one who tends to be an evolutionist. There is an intriguing line from the Book of Mormon during a time period when an abundance of peace and righteousness prevailed between the Nephites and the Lamanites: "And it came to pass that there was no contention in the land, because of the love of God which did dwell in the hearts of the people. . . . There were no robbers, nor murderers, neither were there Lamanites, *nor any manner of -ites*; but they were in one, the children of Christ" (4 Nephi 1:15, 17; emphasis added). President Boyd K. Packer once gave a perceptive commentary on these verses:

> That is worth keeping in mind as we open a discussion on the origin of man, a subject which often leads defenders of opposing views to controversy and to label one another. In the spirit of the Book of Mormon, please, may we drop all labels, all of the "ites," and "isms," and "ists"? Let there be no "evolution*ists*" nor "creation-*ists*" nor any manner of "ists"; just seekers after truth.
>
> One need not be labeled a creationist to accept the hand of God in a separate creation of man. And I surely will not qualify as an evolutionist notwithstanding I believe that many things evolve, for I believe that many other things do not. Views can change, evolve, if you will, toward the truth. I declare the gospel to be both true and inclusive of every true element of any philosophy, indeed the gospel is a fulness of the truth in all of them.[8]

The following statement is from the First Presidency:

> Diversity of opinion does not necessitate intolerance of spirit, nor should it embitter or set rational beings against each other. The Christ taught kindness, patience, and charity. . . .

Our religion is not hostile to real science. That which is demonstrated, we accept with joy; but vain philosophy, human theory and mere speculations of men, we do not accept nor do we adopt anything contrary to divine revelation or to good common sense. But everything that tends to right conduct, that harmonizes with sound morality and increases faith in Deity, finds favor with us not matter where it may be found.[9]

I am somewhat embarrassed to say this, but I almost quit my PhD program that I referenced earlier. It was a five-year program, but I almost quit after the first year. Why did this almost occur? My committee chair was an atheist. Her tone and teachings were almost more than I could bear as we dealt with a lot of theories and philosophies of men with which I disagreed. Had I quit, I could have justified the reason, or so I thought, based on this scripture from 2 Nephi 28:26: "Wo be unto him that hearkeneth unto the precepts of men, and denieth the power of God, and the gift of the Holy Ghost!" I thought to myself, "Oh my goodness! What am I doing studying the precepts of men? I've got to get out of this."

Many former college students have perhaps been in classes where they felt the philosophies being taught were not quite in accordance with their standards and morals. However, if we read on in the account in 2 Nephi, we find this balancing thought in verse 31: "Cursed is he that putteth his trust in man, or maketh flesh his arm, or shall hearken unto the precepts of men, *save their precepts shall be given by the power of the Holy Ghost*" (emphasis added). How does verse 31 help us to understand verse 26? Simply put, we need to be grounded and we need to be committed to our religion, but let's find all the truth we can in other fields, since there are some theories that have been "given by the power of the Holy Ghost."

One former student of mine once shared this insight with me in a class discussion on this topic:

I took a world religions class at the institute, and it's the same type of principle. You look at all the different religions, and they all have a certain truth to it. And as you're learning it, you can say, "Well this kind of proves that religion's a farce," but if you use the gift of the Holy Ghost we've been given, you can see the truthfulness of it. The one thing I like to caution people on a lot of times [is that] when less-actives go, it's during college, because a lot of times they get the information from one source and they stop using God's source.

I love to encourage my students to get all the education they can. We do not need to back down from philosophy, from science, or from anthropology. There are some places where we are going to be challenged academically and morally, but I think that is when we as Latter-day Saints need to be in those courses even more. We need to be more discerning. When we go into those courses we need to be on our feet. We do not take everything at face value, but we need to realize that a lot of it could be great information. Once I finally figured that out, my PhD program became awesome! I started to learn some incredible things from some very gifted instructors. There were times when the Holy Ghost would come and warn me and say, "You know that's not what you believe." We need to be on our toes when we study academically to be able to sift through these things.

There is another interesting scripture in Matthew 23. The Savior is in the later part of His ministry at this point. He is getting down to the last week of His life, and He starts to condemn the Pharisees because they are not focused on the things that matter most. In verse 23, Christ says, "Woe unto you, scribes and Pharisees, hypocrites! For you pay tithe of mint and anise and cummin, and have omitted the weightier matters of the law, judgment, mercy, and faith." Anise is a little tiny seed. What the Savior is saying in his rebuke to the Pharisees is essentially this: "You take care of all the little details in your lives, you Pharisees. All the procedural things, all the administrative things. However, you have neglected the weightier matters: mercy, the spirit . . . those type of things." At the very end of verse 23 it says, "These ought ye to have done, and not to leave the other undone." What is the Savior saying here? If you have to choose between doing educational and vocational activities verses our faith values and commitment to our religion and keeping the commandments, which one do you choose? You choose both!

Let's then examine a few statements from scholars and Church leaders, which serve as an example of balancing science with religion. President Marion G. Romney once said:

> There were no pre-Adamic men in the line of Adam. . . .
>
> I am not a scientist. I do not profess to know anything but Jesus Christ, and him crucified, and the principles of his gospel. If, however, there are some things in the strata of the earth indicating there were men before Adam, they were not the ancestors of Adam.

Adam was the son of God. . . . He did not come up through an unbroken line of organic evolution. There had to be a fall.[10]

Noted academic and BYU scholar Hugh Nibley once gave this helpful observation:

Do not begrudge existence to creatures that looked like men long, long ago, nor deny them a place in God's affection. . . . Nor am I overly concerned as to just when they might have lived, for their world is not our world. They had all gone away long before our people ever appeared. God assigned them their proper times and functions, as he has given me mine—a full-time job that admonishes me to remember his words to the overly eager Moses: "For mine own purpose have I made these things. Here is wisdom and it remaineth in me" (Moses 1:31). It is Adam as my own parent who concerns me. When he walks onto the stage, then and only then the play begins. He opens a book and starts calling out names. They are the sons of Adam, who also qualify as sons of God, Adam himself being a son of God. This is the book of remembrance from which many have been blotted out.[11]

Disclaimer 5: We do not always know what is figurative or literal.

We cannot always tell which things are literal and which things are figurative in the Garden of Eden story and the Creation account. However, we know from scriptures that some things are indeed figurative; and we also know, from modern prophetic voices, that some things are literal. We will mention various example shortly. In the *New Era* magazine from February 2016, the Church released this statement:

Did dinosaurs live and die on this earth long before man came along? There have been no revelations on this question, and the scientific evidence says yes.

The details of what happened on this planet before Adam and Eve aren't a huge doctrinal concern of ours. *The accounts of the Creation in the scriptures are not meant to provide a literal, scientific explanation of the specific processes, time periods, or events involved.*[12]

There may be other aspects that could be both literal and figurative, and, to go further, even some things that have not yet been revealed. We are told Eve was created from Adam's rib. What are we to make of such a bizarre statement? Likewise we are told that Adam was created from the dust of the earth. What exactly does that mean? How are we to understand such a seemingly strange description? We will speak more about this disclaimer, especially as it applies to the next chapter when we discuss certain truths embodied in the Garden of Eden narrative. However, what we want to do now is focus on Adam and Eve and how they came to be. What do the scriptures say, and what do modern prophets declare about these matters?

The Creation of the Earth

There is a pattern that God has established with regards to how He creates not only man but all living organisms—plants, animals, and even the earth itself. In Doctrine and Covenants we encounter a fascinating scripture block that outlines the destiny of the earth and its creation. This outline of the earth's creation could be used as a pattern of the creation of man. It reads:

> And the spirit and the body are the soul of man.
> And the resurrection from the dead is the redemption of the soul.
> And the redemption of the soul is through him that quickeneth all things, in whose bosom it is decreed that the poor and the meek of the earth shall inherit it.
> Therefore, it must needs be sanctified from all unrighteousness, that it may be prepared for the celestial glory. (D&C 88:15–18)

It is interesting to note the subtle transition that takes place between verse 17 and 18: "The meek of the earth shall inherit *it* [the earth]. Therefore, *it* [the earth] must needs be sanctified" (emphasis added). As we continue reading subsequent verses with the context we have establish with regards to the earth, some interesting patterns emerge:

> For after it [the earth] hath filled the measure of its [the earth's] creation, it [the earth] shall be crowned with glory, even with the presence of God the Father;
> That bodies [Heavenly Father's children] who are of the celestial kingdom may possess it [the earth] forever and ever; for, for this intent was it [the earth] made and created, and for this intent are they [Heavenly Father's children] sanctified. . . .
> And again, verily I say unto you, *the earth* abideth the law of a celestial kingdom, for it [the earth] filleth the measure of its [the earth's] creation, and transgresseth not the law—
> Wherefore, it [the earth] shall be sanctified; yea, notwithstanding it [the earth] shall die, it [the earth] shall be quickened again [meaning

resurrected], and shall abide the power by which it [the earth] is quickened, and the righteous [Heavenly Father's children] shall inherit it [the earth].

For notwithstanding they [Heavenly Father's children] die, they also shall rise again, a spiritual body. (D&C 88:19–20, 25–27; emphasis added)

It is as if the earth and all souls thereon have a symbiotic relationship. It is as if we exist together with the same purpose, destiny, and eternal outcome. Likewise, these verses seem to be treating the earth as a living organism; a living being that goes through a process of salvation similar to what we go through.

Now some may wonder on this point how the earth can exercise agency. Interestingly, Brigham Young observed that all God's creations except man obey the law of their Creator. Plants, animals, all forms of creation are obedient to law, including the earth itself (see Helaman 12:6–8). Doctrine and Covenants 77:1 also tells us a little bit about the ultimate destiny of the earth: "What is the sea of glass spoken of by John, 4th chapter, and 6th verse of the Revelation? It is *the earth, in its sanctified, immortal, and eternal state*" (emphasis added). The earth, then, goes through the same creative process that we do. Its ultimate destination is to become a sanctified, eternal sphere.

In Elder Bruce R. McConkie's book *Millennial Messiah*, he says the earth is first created spiritually. It's a celestial creation. He then says the earth is created physically, or in its terrestrial state. After that, once Adam and Eve fall, the earth falls as well and becomes a telestialized earth. Just as we have to overcome the effects of the Fall and go through a process of salvation, Elder McConkie interestingly suggests the earth goes through a form of salvation. Perhaps we do not fully understand this, but he says that the earth's baptism by water occurred with the Flood, and that the earth's baptism by fire will occur at the Second Coming when the wicked are burned, when the earth will be burned as though by fire. After that, the earth becomes a millennial earth and resorts back to a terrestrial state.[13]

The tenth article of faith says that we believe "the earth will be renewed and receive its paradisiacal glory." It will be paradise again; it will be like it was in the days of the Garden of Eden. We sing a hymn in which the phrase appears, "And the earth will appear as the Garden of Eden."[14] We sing another hymn in which there is the phrase, "The lamb and the lion with lie down together without any ire."[15] This happens because there is no death during the Millennium. It is interesting to know that after the thousand-year period where the earth is a millennial earth, the terrestrial earth will have no death. Then, the earth will undergo a type of death, just as we read in section 88, and it will be eventually be resurrected, finally becoming, as we read in section 77, a sanctified, immortal, celestial world. This world will be for us and will belong to us if we become celestial beings.

So the earth goes through a very similar creative process as all of Heavenly Father's children. Joseph Fielding Smith once said, "This earth is a living body. It is true to the law given it. This earth is living and must die. The earth, as a living body, will have to die and be resurrected," and this is just fascinating, "for it too has been redeemed by the blood of Jesus Christ."[16] The Atonement is more than just for sin; it is the very redemptive power that effects all living things. All forms of life that have ever existed will be redeemed by the power of the Atonement.

The Creation of Man

Although there is much we do not know regarding these matters, we must remember our first disclaimer: not everything has been revealed. Heavenly Father seems to have put more emphasis on the creation of man than any of His other creations. So, how did Adam and Eve literally come to be? In the Pearl of Great Price, we encounter an important scripture in our trek to discover the true origin of man: "And *the first man* of all men have I called Adam, which is many" (Moses 1:34; emphasis added). Here we remember our second disclaimer—we have a duty to accept what has been revealed. We will comment on several matters. First of all, we are told that Adam is the first man. What does the phrase, "which is many" mean? Perhaps it refers to the fact that there are many Adams, meaning there are many earths with inhabitants (Moses 7:30). The first man on each earth is called Adam—in other words, *Adam* is not just a person but a special title. The corollary scripture for Eve essentially says the same thing. In Moses 4:26, we learn that "Adam called his wife's name Eve, because she [was] the first of all women, which are many," suggesting that there are many Eves because there are many earths, millions of earths (Moses 7:30). The first woman on each world is called Eve. Eve is the first woman and a title for the first woman on each earth.

A similar verse in Moses 3:7 yields another revealing piece of information: "And I, the Lord God, formed man from the dust of the ground, and breathed into his nostrils the breath of life; and man became a living soul, *the first flesh upon the earth, the first man* also" (emphasis added). Here we are told once again, as in Moses 1:34, that Adam is the first man. But we are also told something else that might sound a little strange. Not only is he the first man, but he is "the first flesh." Now this might sound strange to say, because animals, according to the Creation account, were created before man. However, it may be that "flesh" means something other than physical creation. There is an interesting entry in the Bible Dictionary that is helpful: "The flesh is often spoken of as being a part of our mortal or fallen nature; as opposed to the Spirit, and as needing to be overcome. Since *flesh* often means 'mortality,' Adam is spoken of as the 'first flesh' upon the earth, meaning he was the first mortal on the earth, all things being created in a nonmortal condition and becoming mortal through the Fall of Adam" (Bible Dictionary, "Flesh"). So when it says in Moses 3:7 that Adam was the "first flesh," it does not mean he was the first physical creation, it means he was the first to become mortal.

Then, continuing with the Bible Dictionary entry: "Jesus is the 'Only Begotten of the Father' in the flesh, meaning He is the only one begotten of the Father into mortality" (Bible Dictionary, "Flesh"). This last sentence is interesting. The Savior has many names we call Him by: the Bread of Life, the Living Water, the Messiah, the Lamb of God, and the Firstborn. He has a special title we sometimes use, which is the Only Begotten of the Father in the flesh. Why do we call Christ the Only Begotten of the Father? What do we mean by this doctrine? How is Jesus the only begotten in the flesh? Simply put, He is literally the only one who was begotten by God. If we ask the question, "Who is Jesus Christ's biological mother?" the answer is "Mary." If we ask the question, "Who is Jesus Christ's biological father?" the answer is "God the Father, Elohim." In mortality, Jesus Christ is the only one begotten that way—with Heavenly Father as His biological father. This doctrine is called the doctrine of divine sonship. Christ is the Only Begotten of the Father in the flesh.

Here we should observe that Heavenly Father and Heavenly Mother can create, organize, or beget spirit bodies (see The Family: A Proclamation to the World). Heavenly Father can not only beget a spirit body but can also create (or *beget*) a biological, physical body. Christ is an example of Heavenly Father's ability to beget someone's physical body. For this reason, Christ is called the Only Begotten of the Father in the flesh, meaning into mortality. Adam and Eve got their spirit bodies from

Heavenly Father and Heavenly Mother. But how did Adam and Eve get their physical, biological bodies? Remember, Adam and Eve were begotten before the Fall; Christ was begotten after the Fall. In Luke 3:37–38 we read about Christ's lineage—but this lineage is not just any lineage, it is a biologic lineage: "Which was the son of Mathusala, which was the son of Enoch, which was the son of Jared, which was the son of Maleleel, which was the son of Cainan, which was the son of Enos, which was the son of Seth, which was the son of Adam, *which was the son* of God" (emphasis added).

Elder Bruce R. McConkie commented on these verses as follows: "This statement found also in Moses 6:22 has deep and profound significance and also means what it says. Father Adam came as indicated to this sphere, gaining an immortal body because death had not yet entered the world. Jesus on the other hand was the only begotten in the flesh, meaning into a world of mortality where death already reigned."[17] If Adam and Eve had immortal bodies, what kind of parents would they have had to have? They would have to be immortal!

Here is the official and plain doctrine of the Church from "The Origin of Man" statement in 1909:

> Adam, our first progenitor, "the first man," was, like Christ, preexistent spirit, and like Christ he took upon him an appropriate body, the body of a man, and so became a "living soul." The doctrine of the preexistence—revealed so plainly, particularly in latter days—pours a wonderful flood of light upon the otherwise mysterious problem of man's origin. It shows that man, as a spirit, was begotten and born of heavenly parents and reared to maturity in the eternal mansions of the Father, prior to coming upon the earth in a temporal body to undergo an experience in mortality. It teaches that all men existed in the spirit before any man existed in the flesh and that all who have inhabited the earth since Adam have taken bodies and become souls in like manner.[18]

This means that we got our physical bodies the exact same way Adam and Eve got theirs. Continuing the statement:

> It is held by some that Adam was not the first man upon this earth and that the original human being was a development from lower orders of animal creation. These, however, are the theories of men. The word of the Lord declared that Adam was the "first man of all men" (Moses 1:34), and we are therefore in duty bound to regard him as the primal

parent of our race. . . . Man began life as a human being, in the likeness of our Heavenly Father.

True it is that the body of man enters upon its career as a tiny germ or embryo, which becomes an infant, quickened at a certain stage by the spirit whose tabernacle it is, and the child, after being born, develops into a man. There is nothing in this, however, to indicate that the original man, the first of our race, began life as anything less than a man, or less than the human germ or embryo that becomes a man. . . .

The Church of Jesus Christ of Latter-day Saints, basing its belief on divine revelation, ancient and modern, proclaims man to be the *direct and lineal offspring of Deity.*[19]

Remember Genesis 1:27, "God created man in his own image"? God created the first man the same way we create human life today. Adam and Eve are spirit children of Heavenly Parents for certain, as are we; however, they are also "direct and lineal offspring" of Heavenly Parents as well! What a glorious doctrine to learn that we spiritually and physically descended from Heavenly beings.

The Story of the Rib

Now let us visit another scripture, Genesis 2:7: "And the Lord God formed man of the dust of the ground, and breathed into his nostrils the breath of life; and man became a living soul." The reference to breathing life into Adam's nostrils would appear to be figurative language. Continuing:

And the Lord God said, It is not good that the man should be alone; I will make him an help meet for him.

And out of the ground the Lord God formed every beast of the field, and every fowl of the air; and brought them unto Adam to see what he would call them: and whatsoever Adam called every living creature that was the name thereof.

And Adam gave names to all cattle, and to the fowl of the air, and to every beast of the field; but for Adam there was not found an help meet for him.

And the Lord God caused a deep sleep to fall upon Adam, and he slept: and he took one of his ribs, and closed up the flesh instead thereof;

And the rib, which the Lord God had taken from man, made he a woman, and brought her unto the man.

And Adam said, This is now bone of my bones, and flesh of my flesh: she shall be called Woman, because she was taken out of Man. (Genesis 2:18–23)

With regards to this interesting account of a woman being created from a rib, President Kimball made this plain, clarifying statement: "The story of the rib, of course, is figurative."[20] What does the rib symbolize? It could be said that the rib is designed to be a symbol that, in essence, veils the way in which mankind was really made. In other words, it's a cloaking device to conceal truth from those who are not yet ready to learn the truth. Some make application with the rib symbol by saying it represents man and woman being side by side, equal in partnership. This is a sweet thought, and very appropriate. It is a nice application, but not the best interpretation of the symbol (see Bible Dictionary, "Parables"). This figurative, symbolic rib story actually serves the purpose of veiling the literal doctrine of the origin of man. Parley P. Pratt once perceptively observed this truth as follows:

Thus the holy man was forced again to veil the past in mystery, and in the beginning of his history, assign to man an earthly origin. Man, moulded from the earth, as a brick! A Woman, manufactured from a rib! Thus, parents still would fain conceal from budding manhood the mysteries of procreation, or the sources of life's ever-flowing river, by relating some childish tale of new born life, engendered in the hollow trunk of some old tree, or springing with spontaneous growth like mushrooms from out the heaps of rubbish. O man! When wilt thou cease to be a child in knowledge? Man as we have said, is the offspring of Deity. The entire mystery of the past and future, with regard to his existence, is not yet solved by mortals.[21]

Mother in Heaven

All this talk about Heavenly Parents leads to an interesting question. Every now and then when I teach a lesson on this topic, I'll occasionally have a student ask: "Brother Line, I know we talk about a Mother in Heaven a lot, but She's never mentioned in the scriptures. I know we have one hymn that mentions Her, but it is the only hymn!" Actually, we have three hymns that mention Heavenly Mother (see end of this chapter) and even the scriptures implicitly mention Her at least four times.

In Genesis 2:24, it says, "Therefore shall a man leave his father and his mother, and shall cleave unto his wife: and they shall be one flesh." At this point Adam and Eve are the only man and woman on the earth, and they came from Heavenly Parents—direct, lineal descendants, as we have previously stated. Verse 24 says that Adam left his father *and* his mother, which refers to Heavenly Father and *Heavenly Mother*. The second place in scripture Heavenly Mother is mentioned is in Moses 3:24. This verse has the exact same wording: "Therefore shall a man [Adam] leave his Father [Heavenly Father] and his mother [Heavenly Mother] and cleave unto his wife [Eve] and they shall be one flesh."

Heavenly Mother is also referenced to in Ephesians 5:31–32. Earlier in Ephesians 5:22–23, Paul is talking to the Ephesian Saints about the marriage relationship. He says "wives, submit yourselves unto your own husbands as unto the Lord. The husband is the head of the wife, even as Christ is the head of the church." After thus speaking of the marriage relationship, the Savior compares it to the gospel covenant relationship, and the Church. In this covenant relationship, the husband represents Christ, and the wife represents the Church. Ephesians 5:31 says, "For this cause shall a man leave his father and mother, and shall be joined unto his wife, and they two shall be one flesh." In verse 32 it says, "This is a great mystery: But I speak concerning Christ and the church." Paul is quoting the scripture from Genesis out of context. He is quoting it, and he knows what it means. We know this because he says, "This is a great mystery." A mystery is not something unknowable. It is sacred knowledge that you can only get if you have been appropriately prepared in a place called the temple. What this tells me is that Paul knew the doctrine, but he deliberately takes it out of context, "But I speak of Christ and the church." He is using it to make an application. Heavenly Mother is also mentioned in Abraham 4:27. This verse is a more subtle reference.

The Church has recently released a wonderful essay about this topic that contains this summary declaration: "The Church of Jesus Christ of Latter-day Saints teaches that all human beings, male and female, are beloved spirit children of heavenly parents, a Heavenly Father and a Heavenly Mother. This understanding is rooted in scriptural and prophetic teachings about the nature of God, our relationship to Deity, and the godly potential of men and women. The doctrine of a Heavenly Mother is a cherished and distinctive belief among Latter-day Saints."[22]

Let's also look at Genesis 1:26–27. It is amazing to me the rest of the Christian world has these verses of scripture right in front of them and they do not even see a simple, yet vital, truth which we will now discuss.

In fact, sometimes we, as Latter-day Saints, read these verses and we do not even comprehend what they say: "And God said, Let us make man in our image, after our likeness: and let them have dominion over the fish of the sea, and over the fowl of the air, and over the cattle, and over all the earth, and over every creeping thing that creepeth upon the earth. So *God created man in his own image*, in the image of God created he him; male and female created he them" (emphasis added).

In the Hebrew Bible, the word for God is *Elohim*. In Hebrew, the *-im* at the end of any word makes it plural. However, the King James translators just simply translated it as God, singular. In Abraham 4:27 it reads: "So the Gods went down to organize man in their own image, in the image of the Gods to form they him, male and female to form they them." It is interesting to notice that in Abraham's account it says, "the Gods." Often when we read the book of Abraham we say that when it says "Gods" it refers to Heavenly Father and Jesus Christ, and that is correct. However, President Kimball once said, "God made man in His own image, and certainly he made woman in the image of His wife-partner."[23]

Hymns with Heavenly Mother

"Oh My Father," no. 292

> When I leave this frail existence,
> When I lay this mortal by,
> *Father, Mother*, may I meet you
> In your royal courts on high?
> Then, at length, when I've completed
> All you sent me forth to do,
> With your mutual approbation
> Let me come and dwell with you.

"Oh, What Songs of the Heart," no. 286

> Oh, what songs we'll employ!
> Oh, what welcome we'll hear!
> While our transports of love are complete,
> As the heart swells with joy
> In embraces most dear
> *When our heavenly parents* we meet!
> As the heart swells with joy,
> Oh, what songs we'll employ,
> When our heavenly parents we meet!

"We Meet Again as Sisters," no. 311
>We meet to sing together
>The praises of our Lord,
>To seek our exaltation
>According to his word.
>To ev'ry gospel blessing
>The Lord has turned the key,
>That we, *with heav'nly parents*,
>May sing eternally.

Notes

1. Gordon B. Hinckley, "The Salt Lake Temple," *Ensign*, March 1993, 5–6.
2. I am not the first to suggest such a list of disclaimers in discussing the doctrine of the creation. Although my content and approach is somewhat different, I would acknowledge lectures I have attended that were given by renown BYU scholar Robert L. Millet which served as the impetus in suggesting such a framework for this chapter.
3. Bruce R. McConkie, "Christ and the Creation," *Ensign*, June 1982, 10; emphasis added.
4. Neal A. Maxwell, "The Inexhaustible Gospel" (Brigham Young University Education Week devotional, August 18, 1992), 6, speeches.byu.edu.
5. The problem with this approach is clarified in the Pearl of Great Price, where we learn that a thousand years on earth is as one day, *not with God, but on Kolob,* which is *nigh* (meaning near) unto God (see Abraham 3:1–12). This is to say that time is relative. As one gets closer to the presence of God, time slows down until it stops and past, present, and future all become one. This is not only sound doctrine, it has scientific roots as well in Albert Einstein's theory of special relativity.
6. Furthermore, we one day will die and temporarily lose our physical body but then become resurrected with a perfected body of flesh and bone but without blood. Instead we will have a spiritual substance flowing through our bodies. We will finally be glorified, resurrected, spiritual beings. In Doctrine and Covenants 88:25–27, we read how the earth will be sanctified and quickened, or resurrected, and how "the righteous [you and I] shall inherit it. For notwithstanding they [you and I] die, they also shall rise again, a *spiritual body*" (emphasis added). The fact of the matter is that God is not done creating us; He intends to complete the process, thus fulfilling His

work and glory "to bring to pass the immortality and eternal life of man" (Moses 1:39) and thus making us spiritual beings like He is—glorified, resurrected beings!

7. *Evolution and the Origin of Man* (Provo, UT: Brigham Young University, October 1992).

8. Boyd K. Packer, "The Law and the Light," in *The Book of Mormon: Jacob through Words of Mormon, To Learn with Joy*, eds. Monte S. Nyman and Charles D. Tate Jr. (Provo, UT: Religious Studies Center, Brigham Young University, 1990), 1.

9. "Words in Season from the First Presidency," *Deseret Evening News*, December 17, 1910.

10. Marion G. Romney, in Conference Report, April 1953, 123–24.

11. Hugh Nibley, *Old Testament and Related Studies* (Salt Lake City: Deseret Book, 1986), 82–83.

12. "To the Point," *New Era*, February 2016, 41; emphasis added.

13. Bruce R. McConkie, *The Millennial Messiah: The Second Coming of the Son of Man* (Salt Lake City: Deseret Book, 1982).

14. "Now Let Us Rejoice," *Hymns*, no. 3.

15. "The Spirit of God," *Hymns*, no. 2.

16. Joseph Fielding Smith, *Doctrines of Salvation*, comp. Bruce R. McConkie (1955), 1:72–74.

17. Bruce R. McConkie, *Doctrinal New Testament Commentary* (Salt Lake City: Deseret Book, 1954), 1:95.

18. "The Origin of Man, by the First Presidency of the Church," *Improvement Era*, November 1909, 81.

19. Ibid; emphasis added.

20. Spencer W. Kimball, "The Blessings and Responsibilities of Womanhood," *Ensign*, March 1976, 5.

21. Parley P. Pratt, *Key to the Science of Theology*, 10th ed. (Salt Lake City: Deseret Book, 1948), 50.

22. "Mother in Heaven," lds.org, accessed May 12, 2017, https://www.lds.org/topics/mother-in-heaven.

23. Spencer W. Kimball, *The Teachings of Spencer W. Kimball*, 25.

Four

The First Temple Ever:
The Garden of Eden

Another intriguing and informative part of the temple endowment is the dramatization of the events relating to the account of the Garden of Eden. For the most part, the temple's accounting of Eden follows very similar lines as the accounts in both Genesis and the Pearl of Great Price. Regardless of the account being presented, a question is often raised as to whether Eden is an allegorical story or literal history. Regardless of the answer, the real question that should be asked is this: what is the Lord trying to teach the Saints in this account? What is it, as members of the Church, that we should take away from this sacred instruction?

To answer this question, we must remember this injunction we have already quoted from President Boyd K. Packer: he said that the Atonement "is the very root of Christian doctrine. You may know much about the gospel as it branches out from there, but if you only know the branches and those branches do not touch that root [the Atonement], if they have been cut free from that truth, there will be no life nor substance nor redemption in them." To put this another way, we discovered in the previous chapter that the accounts of the Creation really are not designed to teach us about the Creation, rather, they are designed to teach us about the Atonement of Christ. So with this as our focus, what is it then that the Garden of Eden account is trying to teach us specifically about the Atonement and our relationship to the Savior Jesus Christ?

We know that the temple is highly symbolic; therefore, it would stand to reason that perhaps the Eden account could be likewise symbolic. However, using one of our disclaimers on the Creation from the previous chapter, we could and should say that we cannot always tell which things are figurative and which things are literal. Was Adam's creation from "dust of the earth" a literal expression? Did God actually mix some mud together to form man? Was Eve literally created from a rib? Where there actual physical trees in the Garden of Eden with fruit, some of which could cause a metabolic change in our first parents' bodies? Was there a literal serpent who actually conversed, in spoken word, with humans?

Fortunately, several Church leaders and scholars have weighed in on this issue. In the book *The Man Adam*, the authors surmise that "the scriptural account of the birth of Adam is a sacred metaphor, as is the account of the birth of his eternal companion, Eve."[1] This is confirmed, as stated previously, by President Kimball who said: "The story of the rib, of course, is figurative."[2] Elder Jeffery R. Holland observed that "there was an actual Adam and Eve who fell from an actual Eden. . . . [But] I do not know the details of what happened on this planet before that."[3] Elder Bruce R. McConkie remarked that "as to the Fall itself . . . the account is speaking figuratively."[4]

> How literally do we take the story of the Garden of Eden? This we know: Adam was real. He was as real as Christ. For if Adam was not real the Fall was not real; and if the Fall was not real the Atonement was not real; and if the Atonement was not real Jesus the Christ is not and was not necessary. Of some parts of the Eden story it matters little if we choose to view them as figurative or literal, but of others it is not so. The testimony of Christ, of necessity, embraces the testimony of Adam. Had there been no Eden there could be no Gethsemane; had there been no Eve there could be no Mary; if we have not inherited death from Adam, we have no claim on everlasting life through Christ.[5]

From these statements it would appear that there are both figurative and literal elements in the Garden of Eden account. Likewise, there are some elements we just simply don't know about. But, once again, regardless of one's preferred perspective, what is it the Lord is trying to teach us about Christ and His Atonement? Furthermore, what is the relationship between the story of Eden and temples? In the rest of this chapter, we will look at these questions from a symbolic perspective, using as resources the scriptures to give us interpretations of various elements found in the story of Eden.

Symbols in the Story of Eden

Let's begin with a very rudimentary summary of the events in Eden. In the Garden of Eden there was a tree called the tree of life. This tree had fruit on it, which we will discuss later. God placed Adam and Eve in the Garden and commanded them, among other things, not to partake of the fruit of another tree called the tree of knowledge of good and evil. Adam and Eve gave into temptation and partook of the forbidden fruit of this tree. And so God placed cherubim and a flaming sword around the tree of life so that Adam and Eve could not partake of its fruit.

> For behold, if Adam had put forth his hand immediately, and partaken of the tree of life, he would have lived forever, according to the word of God, having no space for repentance; yea, and also the word of God would have been void, and the great plan of salvation would have been frustrated. (Alma 42:5)

When I was young, I thought this story was a bit strange, and that perhaps is as it should be, especially if one considers, as Elder McConkie taught, that this is a figurative account. So what are the symbols and their associated meanings? We will look at four specific symbols as we try to ascertain the connection that Eden has with the Atonement.

First let's start with the tree of life. It is interesting to note that the tree of life in the book of Genesis is the same tree of life at the beginning of the Book of Mormon. In Lehi's dream, we learn that the tree of life had fruit on it that "was desirable to make one happy. . . . It was most sweet [and] the fruit thereof was white, to exceed all the whiteness" (1 Nephi 8:10–11). Lehi states that "as I partook of the fruit thereof it filled my soul with exceedingly great joy; wherefore, I began to be desirous that my family should partake of it also; for I knew that it was desirable above all other fruit" (1 Nephi 8:12). Later, in 1 Nephi 10, we learn that Lehi's son Nephi was "desirous also that [he] might see, and hear, and know" the same things that his father saw in the dream (1 Nephi 10:17). In 1 Nephi 11, we learn the meaning of the symbol of the tree of life:

> And the angel said unto me: Behold the Lamb of God, yea, even the Son of the Eternal Father! *Knowest thou the meaning of the tree* which thy father saw?

And I answered him, saying: Yea, *it is the love of God*, which sheddeth itself abroad in the hearts of the children of men; wherefore, it is the most desirable above all things. (1 Nephi 11:21–22; emphasis added)

Before concluding a discussion on the meaning of the symbol of the tree of life, it is helpful to know that Nephi's response to the angel is not exactly what Nephi was told by the Spirit earlier in the chapter:

And the Spirit said unto me: Behold, what desirest thou?
And I said: I desire to behold the things which my father saw.
And the Spirit said unto me: Believest thou that thy father saw the tree of which he hath spoken? (1 Nephi 11:2–4)

Notice that of all the symbols in Lehi's dream, the Spirit focuses immediately in on the symbol of the tree. Nephi replies: "And I said: Yea, thou knowest that I believe all the words of my father" (1 Nephi 11:5). What follows next is very interesting: "And when I had spoken these words, the Spirit cried with a loud voice, saying: Hosanna to the Lord, the most high God; for he is God over all the earth, yea, even above all. And blessed art thou, Nephi, *because thou believest in the Son of the most high God*; wherefore, thou shalt behold the things which thou hast desired" (1 Nephi 11:6; emphasis added). To summarize:

Spirit: "Nephi, what do you desire?"
Nephi: "To see what my father saw."
Spirit: "Do you believe in the tree?"
Nephi: "Yes."
Spirit: "That's great—you believe in the Son of God!"

The Spirit continues and confirms this point: "And behold *this thing* [the tree] shall be given unto thee *for a sign* [a sign is a symbol], that after thou hast *beheld the tree* which bore the fruit which thy father tasted, thou *shalt also behold a man* descending out of heaven, and him shall ye witness; and *after ye have witnessed him* [Christ] ye shall bear record that *it* [the tree] is the Son of God" (1 Nephi 11:7; emphasis added). It doesn't say "ye shall bear record that *He* is the Son of God," it says "*it* is the Son of God," *it* referring no doubt to the tree of life. Accordingly, the tree of life is, in the words of the Spirit, Jesus Christ Himself. This differs from Nephi's response as we mentioned earlier, wherein he declares that the tree is "the love of God" (1 Nephi 11:22). Is there a contradiction here? Perhaps not. Maybe Nephi is correct in the sense that his interpretation of the tree, being the love of God, is not so much the technical meaning of the symbol, but perhaps maybe how he feels about the symbol!

Another thought is noteworthy: maybe both answers are correct when one considers this verse from the Bible: "For *God so loved the world, that he gave his only begotten Son,* that whosoever believeth in him should not perish, but have everlasting life" (John 3:16; emphasis added). To summarize, the tree of life is a representation of God's love in the giving of His son, Jesus Christ, to atone for the sins of mankind. In short, the tree is a symbol for the Atonement!

What then does the fruit of the tree of life represent? One way to answer this question is by a logical deduction: Trees produce fruit—what is the ultimate fruit that the Atonement produces? The answer would have to be eternal life. Let's check this logic with the scriptures.

Nephi learns a little later in the account the following: "Wherefore, the wicked are rejected from the righteous, and also from that *tree of life, whose fruit is most precious* and most desirable above all other fruits; yea, and *it is the greatest of all the gifts of God*" (1 Nephi 15:36, emphasis added). But what is the greatest of all the gifts of God? In the Doctrine and Covenants we are told: "And, if you keep my commandments and endure to the end you shall have *eternal life, which gift is the greatest of all the gifts of God*" (D&C 14:7; emphasis added).

In summary, the tree of life represents the Atonement and the fruit represents eternal life. Perhaps this is the source of its name: the tree of eternal life, or simply the tree of life.

Let's now look at some other symbols. From Elder Holland, we learn that Adam and Eve are actual historical people, but we also learn in the temple endowment that they serve as symbols for each one of us. Illustratively, President Boyd K. Packer once said, "What is said in the revelations about the Creation, though brief, is repeated in Genesis, in the Book of Mormon, in Moses, in Abraham, and in the endowment. *We are told it is figurative insofar as the man and the woman are concerned.*"[6] Indeed, the name *Adam*, when used as a masculine noun, literally means "man" or "mankind," usually in a collective context as in humankind.[7] Thus, Adam and Eve, though literal individuals, also can serve as symbols for each individual spirit, male and female, that comes here to earth from the presence of the Father.

What about cherubim and a flaming sword—are they symbolic as well? The answer is yes. How do we know this? The account referenced earlier from Alma 42 gives us a guide to the meaning of this fascinating symbol. Here we find Alma giving counsel to his wayward son, Corianton, who has left his mission labors and, as implied in the text of Alma 39, was guilty of immorality to some degree. The specifics are unclear. In an attempt to reclaim his son, Alma (prior to chapter 42) teaches him vital doctrines about the afterlife, the resurrection, and Christ's Atonement (see Alma 40 and 41). Apparently, Corianton is still struggling with the reasons as to why immorality is wrong, or, at least he is struggling to understand why there is a punishment affixed to this particular sin. Alma, sensing his son's struggle, refers back to the story of the Garden of Eden, with particular emphasis on cherubim and a flaming sword:

> And now, my son, I perceive there is somewhat more which doth worry your mind, which ye cannot understand—which is *concerning the justice of God* in the punishment of the sinner; for ye do try to suppose that it is *injustice* that the sinner should be consigned to a state of misery.
>
> Now behold, my son, I will explain *this thing* [the justice of God in verse 1] unto thee. For behold, after the Lord God sent our first parents forth from the garden of Eden, to till the ground, from whence they were taken—yea, he drew out the man, and he placed at the east end of the garden of Eden, *cherubim, and a flaming sword which turned every way, to keep the tree of life*—
>
> *Now, we see* that the man had become as God, knowing good and evil; and lest he should put forth his hand, and take also of the tree of life, and eat and live forever, the Lord *God placed cherubim and the flaming sword, that he should not partake of the fruit*—
>
> And *thus we see*, that there was a time granted unto man to repent, yea, a probationary time, a time to repent and serve God.
>
> For behold, if Adam had put forth his hand immediately, and partaken of the tree of life, he would have lived forever, according to the word of God, having no space for repentance; yea, and also the word of God would have been void, and the great plan of salvation would have been frustrated.
>
> But behold, it was appointed unto man to die—therefore, as *they were cut off from the tree of life* they should be cut off from the face of the earth—and man became lost forever, yea, they became fallen man.
>
> *And now, ye see* by this that our first parents were *cut off both temporally and spiritually from the presence of the Lord*; and thus we see they became subjects to follow after their own will.
>
> Now behold, it was not expedient that man should be reclaimed from this temporal death, for that would destroy the great plan of happiness.

Therefore, as the soul could never die, and the fall had brought upon all mankind a spiritual death as well as a temporal, that is, *they were cut off from the presence of the Lord*, it was expedient that mankind should be reclaimed from this spiritual death.

Therefore, as they had become carnal, sensual, and devilish, by nature, this probationary state became a state for them to prepare; it became a preparatory state.

And now remember, my son, if it were not for the plan of redemption, (laying it aside) as soon as they were dead their souls were miserable, *being cut off from the presence of the Lord*.

And now, there was no means to reclaim men from this fallen state, which man had brought upon himself because of his own disobedience;

Therefore, *according to justice*, the plan of redemption could not be brought about, only on conditions of repentance of men in this probationary state, yea, this preparatory state; for except it were for these conditions, mercy could not take effect except it should destroy *the work of justice*. Now *the work of justice* could not be destroyed; if so, God would cease to be God.

And *thus we see* that all mankind were fallen, and *they were in the grasp of justice*; yea, *the justice of God, which consigned them forever to be cut off from his presence*.

And now, the plan of mercy could not be brought about except an atonement should be made; therefore God himself atoneth for the sins of the world, to bring about the plan of mercy, to *appease the demands of justice*, that God might be a perfect, just God, and a merciful God also. (Alma 42:1–15; emphasis added)

Several items are worth noting in this account. First, cherubim and a flaming sword are placed so as to keep, to block, or to prevent Adam and Eve from partaking of the tree of life. If we reason this through a little, we can conclude that Adam's transgression resulted in some sort of barrier or blockade being placed so that Adam couldn't get to the tree and its associated fruit, which we understand is a representation of eternal life. When we sin, something or some law kicks in that prevents us from attaining eternal life or exaltation. Verses 7, 9, and 11 all specifically confirm this interpretation, which in essence equates the impediment of cherubim and a flaming sword with being *"cut off both temporally and spiritually from the presence of the Lord."*

Another item worth noting is the repetition of the phrase, "thus we see" or "now we see" or "now behold," which is used in some form at least five times. It is as though Alma is trying to say, "I'm telling you the

Eden story, but I am using it as a symbol to compare this to a spiritual law or reality."

The third thing to note, and perhaps most important, is the use of the word "justice" nine times in various forms. At the outset of the dialogue with his son in verse 1, Alma states that he wants to explain the "justice of God" to him. The kicker is verse 14, which ties the whole symbolism together: "And *thus we see* that all mankind were fallen, and *they were in the grasp of justice*; yea, *the justice of God, which consigned them forever to be cut off from his presence.*"

The symbol of cherubim and a flaming sword is a representation of an abstract spiritual principle called the *law of justice*. In simple terms we would say this: when any of us sins or transgresses (remember we are symbolically Adam and Eve), the law of justice says we cannot have eternal life! Because of sin, justice prevents us, impedes us, and blocks us from returning to our Heavenly Father's presence. Another way to encapsulate this truth can be found in this simple, straightforward declaration from the Doctrine and Covenants: "For I the Lord cannot look upon sin with the least degree of allowance" (D&C 1:31). This is to say that the law of justice is so serious, so exacting, that if we commit just one sin, we are barred forever from God's eternal presence.

The good news is this though: we can get back, and we can have eternal life. This is possible because something or someone was provided by Father from the beginning to satisfy the demands of justice. A plan was given by the Father whereby we could be saved. This merciful plan satisfies the demands of justice; furthermore, "The plan of mercy could not be brought about except an atonement should be made; therefore God himself atoneth for the sins of the world" (Alma 42:15).

In summary, the story of Genesis, relative to the tree of life, is how mankind gets cast away from the tree, while the perspective of the Lehi's dream in the Book of Mormon is how mankind gets back to the tree. However, in Lehi's account there is no cherubim or a flaming sword, thus suggesting that justice has been satisfied through Christ; instead, there is a whole new set of symbols: a path back to the tree; an iron rod that one can hold to not lose their way on the path; activity from the adversary as manifested in the mists of darkness that represent temptation; even a distracting great and spacious building that symbolizes the pride of the world (see 1 Nephi 8). The following chart is a summary of our symbolic view of Eden:

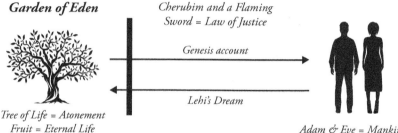

Garden of Eden

Cherubim and a Flaming Swan = Law of Justice

Genesis account

Lehi's Dream

Tree of Life = Atonement
Fruit = Eternal Life

Adam & Eve = Mankind

It is interesting to note how many of these additional symbols in Lehi's dream relate to the Atonement. The path is the gospel path, the only way back to God (see 1 Nephi 8:20–21). The iron rod is the word of God (see 1 Nephi 15:23–24), which means more than just God's "word," rather, it is Christ who is the Word (see John 1). And don't forget the tree of life with its fruit. All of these symbols represent various aspects of Christ's Atonement, which, as we have said, satisfies the demands of justice—or, as Christ once said: "I am the way [the path], the truth [the Word], and the life [the tree of life]" (John 14:6). In other words, He is all of it! His Atonement doesn't just help lift us at the end of our lives, it helps from beginning to end and all the way through our lives as well.

The Tree of Life in Other Scriptures

This same tree of life, as found in Genesis and Lehi's dream, is also found in another story located in Alma 32. In this account, one plants a seed and nourishes the seed with faith. As the seed grows and is continually nourished, it starts to develop into a tree. When fully developed, this tree becomes not just any tree, but a tree of life. This tree likewise has fruit, which is described in similar fashion as the fruit of the tree of life in Lehi's dream:

> And thus, if ye will not nourish the word, looking forward with an eye of faith to the fruit thereof, ye can never pluck of *the fruit of the tree of life.*
>
> But if ye will nourish the word, yea, nourish the tree as it beginneth to grow, by your faith with great diligence, and with patience, looking forward to the fruit thereof, it shall take root; and behold it shall be *a tree springing up unto everlasting life.*
>
> And because of your diligence and your faith and your patience with the word in nourishing it, that it may take root in you, behold, by and by ye shall pluck *the fruit thereof, which is most precious, which is*

sweet above all that is sweet, and which is white above all that is white, yea,
and pure above all that is pure; and ye shall feast upon this fruit even
until ye are filled, that ye hunger not, neither shall ye thirst.

Then, my brethren, ye shall reap the rewards of your faith, and
your diligence, and patience, and long-suffering, waiting for the tree to
bring forth fruit unto you. (Alma 32:40–43; emphasis added)

One interesting thing to note, children in our primary classes often
sing a song about Alma 32. Part of the lyrics are as follows: "Faith is like
a little seed, if planted it will grow."[8] The song is beautiful in its melody
and simple in its message. However, upon closer examination of Alma 32,
a paradox emerges relative to this song: faith is not like a seed—you use
faith to plant the seed. So what does the seed represent? The key to inter-
preting Alma 32 is actually found in Alma 33. As will be seen, the seed
that we are to plant and nourish by our faith is actually six vital and specific beliefs with regards to Jesus Christ and His Atonement:

O my brethren, if ye could be healed by merely casting about your
eyes that ye might be healed, would ye not behold quickly, or would ye
rather harden your hearts in unbelief, and be slothful, that ye would
not cast about your eyes, that ye might perish?

If so, wo shall come upon you; but if not so, then cast about your
eyes and begin to believe in [1] *the Son of God*, [2] that *he will come to*
redeem his people, and that [3] *he shall suffer and die to atone* for their
sins; and that [4] *he shall rise again* from the dead, which shall bring
to pass [5] *the resurrection, that all men shall stand before him*, to be [6]
judged at the last and judgment day, according to their works.

And *now, my brethren, I desire that ye shall plant this word in your*
hearts [meaning the previous six principles or beliefs], and as it [this
seed] beginneth to swell even so *nourish it by your faith* [again, faith
isn't the seed; you nourish the seed by your faith]. And behold, *it will*
become a tree, springing up in you unto everlasting life. (Alma 33:21–23;
emphasis added)

Alma 32 is about how the Atonement "grows up" in you individu-
ally. Jacob 5, the allegory of the olive tree, is another tree of life story. It
is the same tree of life with the same precious fruit (see Jacob 5:74), but
this story is about how the Atonement "grows up" in groups of nations.
Alma 32 is the individualistic approach to the Atonement, and Jacob 5 is
the nationalistic approach. But it is the same tree. All of these tree stories
are symbolic of the Atonement of Jesus Christ.

The Temple and the Garden of Eden

So far we have examined the story of the Garden of Eden (which is dramatized in the temple endowment) in a symbolic perspective (rather than literal) that could be viewed by patrons of the temple to help them learn of and appreciate the Atonement of Jesus Christ, which is the central focus of temple worship. Now we will look at another fascinating connection with the Garden of Eden and temples. Elder James E. Talmage observed that "the Garden in Eden was the first [temple] of earth, for therein did the Lord first speak unto man and make known the Divine law."[9] The concept and view of the Garden of Eden as a temple should not be surprising when one considers the broad definition of a temple, simply being a place where God can commune with mankind, teach them laws, and provide saving ordinances and covenants which enable them to return to the presence of God. In essence, this is the story, albeit symbolic, of the Garden of Eden. "When David plans to build a temple in 2 Samuel 7, the Lord reminds him that 'I have been walking about in a tent [the tabernacle!] for my dwelling.' In a similar manner, the Lord is 'walking' in Eden because *Eden itself was the temple and dwelling place of God.*"[10]

Temples approved of God in all ages thus serve the purpose of instructing mankind (Adam and Eve) the means (the Atonement of Christ that satisfies justice) whereby they may be enabled (through agency of choice and through covenants) to overcome and return to live in the presence of the Father. It could be said that the Garden of Eden thus serves as a pattern for all other temples, including the first man-made temple, which many scholars consider to be the portable Israelite tabernacle, which they carried on their trek through the wilderness. The chart below shows how the tabernacle can be overlaid on our symbolic model of the Garden of Eden that was presented previously.

Holy of Holies   *The Holy Place*

The ancient tabernacle had two rooms: a smaller room called the Holy of Holies and a larger room referred to as the Holy Place. There was a partition that divided these two rooms—this was the veil of the temple, which, interestingly, had cherubim embroidered on it.

It is interesting to consider what happened to the veil of the temple on the day Christ was crucified for the sins of the word: "And, behold, the veil of the temple was rent in twain from the top to the bottom" (Matthew 27:51). This is a fascinating occurrence when one remembers that cherubim and a flaming sword, and by extension the veil of the temple, represent the law of justice. Symbolically, the veil of the temple being rent or parted reminds us again that Christ's Atonement satisfies the demands of justice. It removes that barrier so we can all make it back to Father's presence on conditions of repentance. The imagery is simply beautiful. The interpretation of the veil representing the law of justice finds confirmation in this scriptural reminder from Paul:

> But now in Christ Jesus ye who sometimes were far off are made nigh by the blood of Christ.
>
> For he is our peace, *who hath made both one*, and hath broken down *the middle wall of partition* between us;
>
> Having abolished in his flesh the enmity, even the law of commandments contained in ordinances; for to make in himself of twain one new man, so making peace. (Ephesians 2:13–15; emphasis added)

In both LDS and non-LDS commentaries, "the middle wall" is understood to be the veil of the temple. Thus Christ's Atonement breaks down the middle wall, meaning it satisfies the demands of justice, and it enables mortal man (Adam and Eve) to become "one" again with Heavenly Father.

I am aware that there is another meaning some scholars attach to the symbol of the veil, mainly, that it represents Christ's flesh. This interpretation is based on a nuanced reading of this scripture in Hebrews: "Having therefore, brethren, boldness to enter into the holiest by the blood of Jesus, *By a new and living way, which he hath consecrated for us, through the veil, that is to say, his flesh*; And having an high priest over the house of God" (Hebrews 10:19–21). The view is that "the veil" here is equated with "his flesh." However, when read in context, this passage could be equating the phrase "by a new and living way" with "his flesh"—meaning precisely this: "the new and living way" is through "his flesh" that was sacrificed for us in order that the law of justice could be satisfied, thus enabling us to enter back "through the veil" into His divine presence. Thus the meaning of the symbol of the veil, when considering all the accounts in Hebrews, Ephesians, and Alma 42, is more accurately portrayed and appropriately applied as representing the law of justice as has been said.

It is interesting to consider the symbol of the veil with its associated interpretation when considering modern temples today. Mainly, that when one approaches the veil, they cannot just go through alone, even if they are perfect in word. No, we have to have someone there with us who enables us to get through the veil back into the presence of the Father. Once again, we all need the Savior's Atonement to get past that which is blocking us or keeping us from the divine presence.

Let us look at some additional symbolism. The ancient tabernacle had various items that served as reminders to the Israelites as to how their trek back into His eternal presence was to be conducted.

Holy of Holies   *The Holy Place*

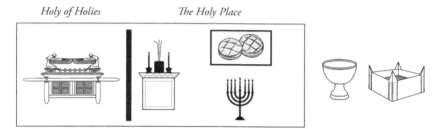

The ark of the covenant was the only item in the Holy of Holies. It contained, among other things, the tablets of the law, even the Ten Commandments. Next to the veil in the Holy Place was the altar of incense. Also in the Holy Place were two other items: the seven-pronged candlestick called the menorah, and the table of shewbread. Outside there were two additional items: one was the great wash basin; the other was the great sacrificial altar. In Hebrews chapters 8 through 10, Paul reminds us that the tabernacle is a pattern of the heavens. In the layout above, you can see how each area could represent a different kingdom of glory: the celestial (Holy of Holies), the terrestrial (Holy Place), and the telestial (the outer courtyard with the basin and altar). In temples today, we also have rooms that represent these different kingdoms or degrees of glory.

The ancient tabernacle likewise serves as a pattern we all can follow through our lives as we use the Savior's Atonement to get back to Heavenly Father's presence. For the ancient Israelites, the temple service always commenced with the sacrificial altar and progressed through the temple, ultimately culminating with the once-a-year visit by the High Priest of Israel to the Holy of Holies on the Day of Atonement, known to the Jews as Yom-Kippur. If we start, as they started, and move item by item to the Holy of Holies, an interesting pattern emerges.

First, the sacrificial altar can serve as a reminder that we all first need to have faith in the atoning sacrifice of Jesus Christ. Second, the altar can also serve as a reminder that we need to offer our own sacrifice of a broken heart and contrite spirit (see 3 Nephi 9:19–20). This sacrifice could also be termed *repentance*, where we surrender or sacrifice our will to God's.

Third, we come to the great wash basin that was filled with water. This place of ceremonial cleansing, in which the priests of Israel would engage, undoubtedly can likewise remind each of us of the washing we receive when we enter into the waters of baptism. It is interesting to note that the baptismal font in temples today include the oxen, which is reminiscent of the basin in ancient Israel.

Fourth, we encounter the light of the menorah, which can remind us that after baptism we can receive the gift of the Holy Ghost, the light that guides each of us as members of Christ's Church. Notice that the menorah is not outside but inside the temple. This could remind us that we are not just "given" the Holy Ghost when we are confirmed members of the Church. No, we are given this command: "I say unto you, receive the Holy Ghost," suggesting to us that we need to leave the outside influences of the world and deliberately choose to enter into the light and into holiness. Also, Aaronic priests can baptize, but only a Melchizedek priesthood holder can confirm someone a member of the Church. We have the outward, or lower, ordinances of the Aaronic Priesthood; and the inward or higher ordinances of the Melchizedek priesthood. These first four steps as we have outlined can serve to remind us thus of the first principles and ordinances of the gospel (see the fourth article of faith).

The table of shewbread also contained wine, which the Aaronic priests of Israel would change once a week on the Sabbath day. This could remind us of the sacrament that we take once a week; the emblems of the bread and wine reminding us not only of Christ and His Atonement but also of the covenants we made at baptism. Next we come to the altar of incense before the veil. The incense was a reminder of prayers ascending to heaven. For those who are endowed, this is a straightforward reminder—coming to an altar before the veil to pray to God. In essence, this is what the endowment is all about: learning how to pray to God, to come before the veil, to make covenants, so we may enter back into his presence one day.

The final item of the temple is the ark of the covenant, which, as we have said, was the only item in the Holy of Holies, representing the divine, celestial presence of God. Once a year, and only once a year, the High Priest would take the blood of the sin offering on the Day of Atonement and would walk with it into the Holy Place and pass through the veil. He was the only one that could do this, and this was the only day of the year it could be done.

Paul tells us in Hebrews that the High Priest of Israel was a symbol for Christ. Only Christ can pass the veil (the law of justice) in and of Himself. He does this so He can then satisfy the demands of justice and let us in. Once inside the Holy of Holies, the High Priest would sprinkle the blood of the sin offering on top of the mercy seat, which was the covering for the ark of the covenant. The mercy seat was in essence a cap that had two winged cherubs on it, facing each other. The meaning of these two cherubs is not known, according to the LDS Bible Dictionary. Perhaps that is as it should be. Thus, these two cherubs could represent any two individuals in the celestial presence, facing each other at this third altar, with the blood of the sin offering between them—perhaps reminding us of the highest ordinance in the house of God, even celestial marriage . . . thus completing our trek back into God's presence to partake of eternal life, which brings us full circle, back to the tree of life!

Conclusion

As we have said, the temple is highly symbolic. It is symbolic of Christ and the outcomes of His Atonement, even eternal life. In my experience as a Church educator and as a bishop, I have often seen some interesting reactions from people that go through endowment sessions. One reaction is, "This is weird." The other reaction is, "This is boring." Neither reaction need be the case if the symbolism were understood. The temple is a more intricate metaphor than what we would sometimes suspect. To understand it better, we must, as students of the temple, use both our hearts and our minds. As it says in section 88 of the Doctrine and Covenants, we learn "by study and also by faith" (D&C 88:118).

The story in the book of Genesis about trees, ribs, and cherubim is not just a silly, archaic story. It is a story with ample meaning, with teachings of great import and deep symbolism. In some ways the symbolism is also very simple. The symbols of the temple, including the highly symbolic story of the Garden of Eden, are much like the parables of Jesus. Applicably, Elder Bruce R. McConkie once stated: "Our Lord used parables [which are in essence symbolic stories] on frequent occasions during his ministry to teach gospel truths. His purpose, however, in telling these short stories was not to present the truths of his gospel in plainness so that all his hearers would understand. Rather it was so to phrase and hide the doctrine involved that only the spiritually literate would understand it, while those whose understandings were darkened would remain in darkness. It is never proper to teach any person more than his spiritual capacity qualifies him to assimilate."[11]

Notes

1. Joseph Fielding McConkie in *The Man Adam*, eds. Robert Millet and Joseph Fielding McConkie (Salt Lake City: Bookcraft, 1990), 26.
2. Spencer W. Kimball, "The Blessings and Responsibilities of Womanhood," *Ensign*, March 1976, 71.
3. Jeffrey R. Holland, "Where Justice, Love, and Mercy Meet," *Ensign*, May 2015, 105.
4. Bruce R. McConkie, "Christ and the Creation," *Ensign*, June 1982, 14.
5. Joseph Fielding McConkie in *The Man Adam*, eds. Robert Millet and Joseph Fielding McConkie (Salt Lake City: Bookcraft, 1990), 27.
6. Boyd K. Packer, "The Law and the Light," (address given at the Book of Mormon Symposium, Brigham Young University, October 30, 1988); emphasis added.
7. See Wilhelm Gesenius and Samuel Prideaux Tregelles, *Gesenius's Hebrew and Chaldee Lexicon to the Old Testament Scriptures* (J. Wiley & Sons, 1893), xiii.
8. "Faith," *Children's Songbook*, 96–97.
9. James E. Talmage, *The House of the Lord: A Study of Holy Sanctuaries Ancient and Modern* (Salt Lake City: The Church of Jesus Christ of Latter-day Saints, 1912), 15.
10. G. K. Beale and Mitchell Kim, *God Dwells Among Us: Expanding Eden to the Ends of the Earth* (Downers Grove, IL: InterVarsity Press, 2014), 18; emphasis added.
11. Bruce R. McConkie, *Mormon Doctrine*, 2nd ed. (Salt Lake City: Deseret Book, 1966), 393.

Five

Symbolic Trees of the
Garden of Eden

Doth a fountain send forth at the same place sweet water and bitter?
(James 3:11)

*I*n this chapter,[1] we continue to examine the symbolic trees of Eden that we encounter in the temple. Our hope is to come to a deeper and richer understanding of the symbolism of these trees and their associated fruit; and, by so doing, to develop a deeper and more meaningful appreciation for this specific aspect of temple symbolism.

Regarding the tree of life, a peculiar verse of scripture in 2 Nephi chapter 2 may go unnoticed at first glance. But a closer look reveals a phrase that seems a bit confusing and almost contradictory. This verse lies between two powerful and succinct concepts—one teaching the doctrine of the Atonement (verse 3–10) and the other the doctrine of the Fall (verses 16–25). In 2 Nephi 2:15, we read the following:

> And to bring about his eternal purposes in the end of man, after he had created our first parents, and the beasts of the field and the fowls of the air, and in fine, all things which are created, it must needs be that there was an opposition; *even the forbidden fruit in opposition to the tree of life; the one being sweet and the other bitter.* (emphasis added)

The items of interest here are the different fruits. One is the forbidden fruit, obviously from the tree of knowledge of good and evil; and the other, though not explicitly stated, is the fruit of the tree of life. At least two points of view become apparent when one seeks to make an interpretation of each type of fruit. First, a textual logic seems to indicate that the forbidden fruit is the one being referred to as "sweet" since it is mentioned first and then so described in the latter part of the sentence. Similarly, the fruit of the tree of life would appear to be, according to the text, the one that is "bitter" for the same reasons described previously. However, there is a second possible meaning. When viewed from a chiastic perspective, the fruit of the tree of life could be the one that is sweet, while the forbidden fruit would be bitter.[2] In light of these two possibilities, it is interesting to note President Harold B. Lee's commentary: "[God] set the tree of knowledge of good and evil in opposition to the tree of life. The fruit of the one which was 'bitter' was the tree of life, and the forbidden fruit was the one which was 'sweet' to the taste."[3] President Lee's interpretation of this scriptural verse clearly coincides with the first point of view.

What is the predicament then? Simply stated, one would think that the fruit of the tree of life would be the fruit that is sweet as Lehi explicitly states in 1 Nephi 8, not bitter as the same Lehi seems to later indicate in 2 Nephi 2. The questions that this chapter will seek to answer are these: Is the fruit of the tree of life bitter, or sweet, or both? What are the implications from understanding this scriptural and doctrinal concept?

Two Trees and Two Fruits

It might be asked how the fruit of the tree of life can be both sweet and bitter. Interestingly, the scriptural account of the Garden of Eden in Genesis 3:6 seems to concur with Lehi's assessment that the forbidden fruit is actually the one that is sweet:

> And when the woman saw that *the tree was good* for food, and that *it was pleasant* to the eyes, and a *tree to be desired* to *make one wise*, she took of the fruit thereof, and did eat, and gave also unto her husband with her; and he did eat. (emphasis added)

Logic seems to indicate that if the fruit of the tree of life in Lehi's vision is sweet, then the forbidden fruit must therefore be bitter. It should be noted that the partaking of the forbidden fruit could be considered a "sweet" thing (i.e., good) in a certain sense. Later on in 2 Nephi 2 (which, again, seems to be referring to the forbidden fruit as the "sweet" fruit), we read the following: "Adam fell that men might be; and men are, that they might have joy" (verse 25). The action of partaking the forbidden fruit perhaps is bitter, but the long-term ramifications are sweet. That is to say, the partaking of the forbidden fruit was tactically a fault but strategically a success! Or, as Elder Dallin H. Oaks has declared, the fall "was formally a transgression, but eternally a glorious necessity to open the doorway toward eternal life."[4] Said Eve to Adam: "Were it not for *our transgression* we never should have had seed, and never should have known good and evil, and the *joy of our redemption*" (Moses 5:11; emphasis added). This vital and empowering principle is one of the key doctrines taught in the temple endowment and underscores the relationship between the doctrine of the Fall and the doctrine of the Atonement. Once again, the symbols of the temple, if seen in proper perspective, can teach us amazing truths regarding Christ's Atonement and the redemption He offers us. Elder Orson F. Whitney explained: "The Fall had a two-fold direction—downward, yet forward. It brought man into the world and set his feet upon progression's highway."[5] Despite these observations, there is still the dilemma of the description of the fruit of the tree of life in Lehi's dream (1 Nephi 8) wherein the fruit is described as actually the one that is sweet. How might this be so?

Perspectives and Implications

Perhaps the answer to this simple dilemma can be found in a profound yet simple teaching from the endowment ceremony as it relates to the Garden of Eden. The corollary scriptural account as found in the Pearl of Great Price, specifically, Moses 4:12, which reads almost identical to its counterpart in Genesis 3:6, has two very interesting albeit small changes:

> And when the woman saw that the tree was good for food, and *that it became pleasant* to the eyes, and a tree to be desired *to make her wise*, she took of the fruit thereof, and did eat, and also gave unto her husband with her, and he did eat. (emphasis added)

The phrase from Genesis "was pleasant" is changed to "became pleasant"—perhaps suggesting that the forbidden fruit really isn't sweet at all. The serpent made it appear that way. In the end, sin never is sweet, or, as Alma would say: "wickedness never was happiness" (Alma 41:10). The following chart can serve as a model for what is being suggested. On the surface, Satan makes sin and transgression appealing through entice- ments, but in reality these things are bitter. Such is the assessment of King Benjamin where he equates the forbidden fruit with the bitter realities of guilt, misery, and endless torment (Mosiah 3:25–26). Likewise, Alma equates the partaking of the forbidden fruit with being "a lost and fallen people" (Alma 12:22).

	On the Surface	*Reality*
Forbidden Fruit	Sweet (by deception)	Bitter
Fruit of Tree of Life	Bitter (by deception)	Sweet

There may be times when the initial taste of sin is sweet or desirable to an individual. But once wickedness and perversion are swallowed and processed by our eternal spirits, we sadly discover the bitter reality of our choice. Although sin is and always will be bitter, we can experience a momentary pleasure or rush of seeming happiness or fun. These disguised delights and fleeting flashes of excitement might even last more than a few moments—perhaps even a day, a week, or longer. "But if it be not built upon my gospel, and is built upon the works of men, or upon the works of the devil, verily I say unto you *they have joy in their works for a season*, and by and by the end cometh, and they are hewn down and cast into the fire, from whence there is no return" (3 Nephi 27:11; emphasis added). It might sound strange that God would permit a person to "have joy" in sinning, albeit for a short season. One might think that perhaps an immediate divine punishment would be the best response to sin and sinners. President Spencer W. Kimball once gave this wise counsel:

> Now, we find many people critical when a righteous person is killed, a young father or mother is taken from a family, or when violent deaths occur. Some become bitter when oft-repeated prayers seem unanswered. Some lose faith and turn sour when solemn administrations by holy men seem to be ignored and no restoration seems to come from repeated prayer circles. But if all the sick were healed, if all the righteous were protected and the wicked destroyed, the whole program of the Father would be annulled and the basic principle of the gospel, free agency, would be ended.
>
> *If pain and sorrow and total punishment immediately followed the doing of evil, no soul would repeat a misdeed. If joy and peace and rewards were instantaneously given the doer of good, there could be no evil—all would do good and not because of the rightness of doing good.* There would be no test of strength, no development of character, no growth of powers, no free agency, no Satanic controls.

Should all prayers be immediately answered according to our selfish desires and our limited understanding, then there would be little or no suffering, sorrow, disappointment, or even death; and if these were not, there would also be an absence of joy, success, resurrection, eternal life, and godhood.[6]

Conversely, Satan would have us believe that the fruit of the tree of life is bitter, not sweet. Although the fruit of the tree is ultimately eternal life, all sons or daughters of God can taste small portions of this precious fruit as they adhere to principles of righteous living throughout their lives. Scripture study, prayer, tithes and offerings, service, Sabbath worship—these are all activities that the adversary would have us believe are bitter, unwanted, profitless, boring, and meaningless pursuits. Perhaps to the spiritually dead, such is the case. But "to the hungry soul every bitter thing is sweet" (Proverbs 27:7).

After all is said and done, "we see the end of him who perverteth the ways of the Lord; and thus we see that the devil will not support his children at the last day, but doth speedily drag them down to hell" (Alma 30:60). Thus, depending on one's perspective, the fruit from either tree can be perceived as both bitter and sweet. The important thing then, is to have the proper perspective. Perhaps this is what Isaiah was alluding to when he emphatically declared: "Woe unto them that call evil good, and good evil; that put darkness for light, and light for darkness; that put *bitter for sweet*, and *sweet for bitter!*" (Isaiah 5:20; emphasis added; cf. 2 Nephi 15:20).

The Close Proximity of the Bitter and Sweet

Although we should never mistake *sweet* for *bitter*, we should understand that these two adjectives are nonetheless intertwined and closely related to each other. It is interesting to note the nearness of the symbolic *tree of life* in Lehi's dream to another symbol in his dream, mainly, the *river water*: "And as I cast my eyes round about, that perhaps I might discover my family also, I beheld a river of water; and it ran along, and *it was near* the tree of which I was partaking the fruit" (1 Nephi 8:13; emphasis added). In Nephi's subsequent vision, the river of water is a representation of the depths of hell and is described as containing "filthy water" (1 Nephi 12:16) that proceeds from a fountain.

Another interesting item in Lehi's dream is the nearness of the filthy river to the iron rod that leads to the tree of life and its associated fruit:

"And I beheld a rod of iron, and it extended along the bank of the river, and led to the tree by which I stood" (1 Nephi 8:19). Later, in Nephi's vision, we learn the symbolism of the iron rod as Nephi answers questions from his brothers: "And they said unto me: What meaneth the rod of iron which our father saw, that led to the tree? And I said unto them that it was the word of God; and whoso would hearken unto the word of God, and would hold fast unto it, they would never perish; neither could the temptations and the fiery darts of the adversary overpower them unto blindness, to lead them away to destruction" (1 Nephi 15:23–24).

Thus it is apparent from Lehi's symbolic dream that the river of filthy water runs alongside the iron rod all the way to the tree of life. The point in this analysis is to highlight the proximity of the *sweet* to that which is *bitter*. These two are always near to each other, that is, they run alongside each other (1 Nephi 8:13) from beginning to end! This geographical and symbolic occurrence points to a literal and sobering reality here in mortality. Although one might be holding to the iron rod and safely walking the straight and narrow path, sin is only a step away. The same is true with any form of bitterness, whether through sin or natural trials and adversity—there always seems to be a divine deference that allows joy and misery to incessantly be on the heels of each other. Elder Neal A. Maxwell once said:

> So often in life a deserved blessing is quickly followed by a needed stretching. Spiritual exhilaration may be quickly followed by a vexation or temptation. Were it otherwise, extended spiritual reveries or immunities from adversity might induce in us a regrettable forgetfulness of others in deep need. *The sharp, side-by-side contrast of the sweet and the bitter is essential* until the very end of this brief, mortal experience.[7]

Similarly, Brigham Young taught: "Will sin be perfectly destroyed? No, it will not, for it is not so designed in the economy of heaven. Do not suppose that we shall ever in the flesh be free from temptations to sin. We shall more or less feel the effects of sin so long as we live and finally have to pass the ordeals of death."[8]

We see this pattern repeated so often in the scriptures, especially with the tutoring and training of prophets, the "sharp, side-by-side" contrast of good and evil, that is—Joseph Smith and the First Vision, Moses in the Pearl of Great Price (see Moses 1), and even the vision of God and Christ in Doctrine and Covenants section 76 is followed immediately by the vision of Lucifer and the one third of the hosts of heaven in the same section—the list of pedagogical foils goes on. Elder John A. Widtsoe declared that "truth and untruth, travel together side by side. Light and darkness both offer themselves to the seeker after truth, one to bless, the other to destroy mankind. Whenever a man sets out to seek truth, he will for a time be over-taken by evil. No seeker after truth is, therefore, ever free from temptation, from evil power."[9] This perplexing truth is declared and described beauti-fully in a poem by William Blake:

> Joy and Woe is woven fine.
> A Clothing for the Soul divine.
> Under every grief and pine,
> Runs a joy with silken twine. . . .
>
> It is right it should be so.
> Man was made for Joy and Woe.
> And when this we rightly know
> Through the World we safely go.[10]

With such close proximity between the sweet and bitter we must be ever vigilant. How do we avoid the filthy water? True it is that we cannot escape this world of sin. We perhaps can avoid sinning to some degree, but as President Young states, we cannot ever avoid the temptation to sin. We must be in the world, but not of the world. A wonderful principle found at the conclusion of Nephi's vision gives us a clue as to perhaps how this can be accomplished.

While explaining to Laman and Lemuel the symbols of his vision (and his father's dream), Nephi gives the following instruction regarding the meaning of the river of water: "And I said unto them that the water which my father saw was filthiness; *and so much was his mind swallowed up in other things that he beheld not the filthiness of the water*" (1 Nephi 15:27; emphasis added). One of the keys to avoiding the ever-encroaching river of sin in our lives is to have our minds and actions focused on many other good and uplifting *things*—to the point where there is no time or interest in sin itself. It can be as though sin is not even there. Cognitively we may know it is there, but we are not perplexed or filled with undue anxiety over its existence. As Elder David A. Bednar has taught, being "endowed with agency, we are agents, and we primarily are to act and not only to be acted upon."[11]

How Bitter Is Bitter?

Having established that we should never mistake sweet for bitter, or bitter for sweet; we thus face an interesting dilemma here in mortality wherein we cannot avoid tasting the bitter, while likewise experiencing the sweet. Both of these realities, as has been stated, appear intertwined and inextricably linked together.

> And the Lord spake unto Adam, saying: Inasmuch as thy children are conceived in sin, even so when they begin to grow up, sin conceiveth in their hearts, and they taste the bitter, that they may know to prize the good.
>
> And it is given unto them to know good from evil; wherefore they are agents unto themselves. (Moses 6:55–56)

In these verses, sin is definitely equated with bitterness. But it is interesting to note that we apparently are to taste the bitter here in mortality in order "to prize the good" (i.e., to taste the sweet). A passage from the Doctrine and Covenants seems to concur with Moses:

> And it must needs be that the devil should tempt the children of men, or they could not be agents unto themselves; for if they never should have bitter they could not know the sweet—
>
> Wherefore, it came to pass that the devil tempted Adam, and he partook of the forbidden fruit and transgressed the commandment, wherein he became subject to the will of the devil, because he yielded unto temptation. (D&C 29:39–40)

Although it is a scriptural truth that "all have sinned, and come short of the glory of God" (Romans 3:23), are we to infer that in order to know and achieve righteousness, we first must experience sin? Paul seems to clarify that such might not be case: "What shall we say then? Shall we continue in sin, that grace may abound? God forbid" (Romans 6:1–2). President Kimball's words are instructive:

> Resistance to sin is better than repentance. Another error into which some transgressors fall, because of the availability of God's forgiveness, is the illusion that they are somehow stronger for having committed sin and then lived through the period of repentance. This simply is not true. That man who resists temptation and lives without sin is far better off than the man who has fallen, no matter how repentant the latter may be. The reformed transgressor, it is true, may be more understanding of one who falls into the same sin, and to that extent perhaps more helpful

in the latter's regeneration. But his sin and repentance have certainly not made him stronger than the consistently righteous person.[12]

Obviously, since we all sin, Christ is the spiritually strongest of all of Father's spirit children; He is the only really consistently righteous person who has or ever will live (see 1 Nephi 10:6; D&C 82:2, 6; Romans 3:10–12, 23). However, this is not to say that He is unacquainted with the bitterness of trials, grief, affliction, and temptation. Interestingly, it is because of His perfect righteousness that He understands the bitterness of sin so much more than the rest of humanity. C. S. Lewis's words are memorable:

> A silly idea is current that good people do not know what temptation means. This is an obvious lie. Only those who try to resist temptation know how strong it is. After all, you find out the strength of the [opposing] army by fighting against it, not by giving in. You find out the strength of a wind by trying to walk against it, not by lying down. A man who gives in to temptation after five minutes simply does not know what it would have been like an hour later. That is why bad people, in one sense, know very little about badness. They have lived a sheltered life by always giving in.[13]

To be sure, sin is bitter. But is bitterness always the same thing as sin? Trials are definitely part of our mortal probation and we must experience "opposition in all things" in order to grow toward eternal life. Therefore we must experience the bitter in order to prize the sweet. But, once again, must we experience the bitterness of sin? Elder Bruce C. Hafen once observed: "As part of an eternal plan, our Father placed us in this world subject to death, sin, sorrow, and misery—ALL of which serve the eternal purpose of letting us taste the bitter that we may learn to prize the sweet."[14] On another occasion, he remarked:

> We might think of the degree of our personal fault for the bad things that happen in our lives as a continuum ranging from sin to adversity, with the degree of our fault dropping from high at one end of the spectrum to zero at the other. At the "sin" end of the continuum, we bear grave responsibility, for we bring the bitter fruits of sin fully upon ourselves. But at the other end of the spectrum, marked by "adversity," we may bear no responsibility at all. The bitterness of adversity may come to us, as it did to Job in the Old Testament, regardless of our actual, conscious fault.

Along this fault-level continuum, between the poles of sin and adversity, lie such intermediate points as unwise choices and hasty judgments. In these cases, it may be unclear just how much personal fault we bear for the bitter fruits we may taste or cause others to taste. Bitterness may taste the same, whatever its source, and it can destroy our peace, break our hearts, and separate us from God. Could it be that the great "at-one-ment" of Christ could put back together the broken parts and give beauty to the ashes of experience such as this?

I believe that it does, because *tasting the bitter in all its forms* is a deliberate part of the great plan of life.[15]

We might ask if our bitter moments in life, whether through sin or adversity, have helped us to become humble. Have our fiery trials served the purpose of softening our hearts? We know we can either be humble because we so choose or because we are compelled to be so (see Alma 32). Elder Maxwell once said: "The returning prodigals are never numerous enough, but regularly some come back from 'a far country'. Of course, it is better if we are humbled 'because of the word' rather than being compelled by circumstances, yet the latter may do! Famine can induce spiritual hunger."[16] Whether the bitter fruit is through sin or adversity (or a combination of both), it should be sufficient to help us appreciate the sweet fruits of virtue, benevolence, and righteous living.

Conclusion

The temple endowment contains an entrancing narrative relative to the Garden of Eden, which, when seen symbolically, can teach many powerful life lessons, not only about Christ's infinite Atonement but also the necessity of learning and applying His redemptive powers through the experience of the sweet and bitter. It could be said that this mortal probation is an experiential escalator. It is a realm of rigorous reality, tempering trials, and tough learning. The school of "hard-knocks" is always in session. Our divine dean has given the demanding directive to all of Adam and Eve's children: "And we will prove them herewith, to see if they will do all things whatsoever the Lord their God shall command them" (Abraham 3:25). Although we might seek to skip class at times, we eventually discover the eternal truth that "it must needs be, that there is an opposition in all things" (2 Nephi 2:11). Although some lessons are bitter, we rejoice in those moments that are sweet. We soon realize, if we are willing, that these two existing realities (the bitter and the sweet) are not mutually exclusive courses that can be taken through independent study; rather, they are reinforcing and complementary classes that must be taken simultaneously—for *"all these things* shall give [us] experience, and shall be for [our] good" (D&C 122:7; emphasis added). Elder Maxwell perceptively observed that "God [is not] a kindly grandfather who would indulge mankind in whatever they wish to do. . . . Ours is a loving Father who will, if necessary, let come to each of us some harsh life experiences, that we might learn that his love for us is so great and so profound that he will let us suffer, as he did his Only Begotten Son in the flesh, that his and our triumph and learning might be complete and full."[17] May we learn our lessons well and always hold to the iron rod, seeking constantly for the fruit of that sacred knowledge and experience that is "most precious, which is sweet above all that is sweet, and which is white above all that is white, yea, and pure above all that is pure" (Alma 32:42). May these precious symbolic teachings from the temple constantly point us to Christ, His Atonement, and the power and joy of His redemption.

Notes

1. The text of this chapter was originally published in C. Robert Line, "Bitter and Sweet: Dual Dimensions of the Tree of Life," in *The Things Which My Father Saw: Approaches to Lehi's Dream and Nephi's Vision*, eds. Daniel L. Belnap, Gaye Strathearn, and Stanley A. Johnson (Provo, UT: Religious Studies Center, Brigham Young University; Salt Lake City: Deseret Book, 2011); reused with permission.

2. Chiasmus is a form of writing or speech in which various words or clauses are related to each other through a reversal of structure (i.e., inverted parallelism).

3. Harold B. Lee, *Stand Ye in Holy Places* (Salt Lake City: Deseret Book, 1974), 364.

4. Dallin H. Oaks, "The Great Plan of Happiness," *Ensign*, November 1993, 73.

5. Orson F. Whitney, in *Cowley and Whitney on Doctrine,* comp. Forace Green (Salt Lake City: Bookcraft, 1963), 287.

6. Spencer W. Kimball, "Tragedy or Destiny," *Improvement Era*, March 1966, 180, 210; emphasis added.

7. Neal A. Maxwell, "Enduring Well," *Ensign*, April 1997, 7; emphasis added.

8. Brigham Young, in *Journal of Discourses*, 10:173.

9. John A. Widtsoe, "The Significance of the First Vision" (Joseph Smith Memorial Sermon, Logan Institute, December 8, 1946).

10. William Blake in *The Complete Poetry and Prose of William Blake*, ed. David V. Erdman (New York: Doubleday, 1988), 494–495.

11. David A. Bednar, "Seek Learning by Faith," *Ensign*, September 2007, 63; see also 2 Nephi 2:14.

12. Spencer W. Kimball, *The Miracle of Forgiveness* (Salt Lake City: Bookcraft, 1969), 357.

13. C. S. Lewis, *Mere Christianity*, rev. ed. (1952; repr., New York: HarperOne, 2015), 143.

14. Bruce C. Hafen, "Elder Bruce C. Hafen Speaks on Same-Sex Attraction," (address given at the Evergreen International annual conference, September 19, 2009), mormonnewsroom.org.

15. Bruce C. Hafen, "Beauty for Ashes: The Atonement of Jesus Christ," *Ensign*, April 1990; emphasis added.

16. Neal A. Maxwell, "The Tugs and Pulls of the World," *Enisgn*, November 2000, 36.

17. Neal A. Maxwell, in *Charge to Religious Educators*, 3rd ed. (Salt Lake City: The Church of Jesus Christ of Latter-day Saints, 1994), 97.

Six

Sacred Clothing and Christ's Atonement

Zion must increase in beauty, and in holiness, . . . and put on her beautiful garments. (D&C 82:14)

What are these which are arrayed in white robes? And whence came they? . . . And he said to me, These are they which came out of great tribulation, and have washed their robes, and made them white in the blood of the Lamb. (Revelation 7:13–14)

Thus far we have focused on the fact that all things point to Christ, and so it is with all things that pertain to the temple (see Moses 6:62–63, 2 Nephi 11:4, and Jacob 4:5). As we have established already in previous chapters, this is specifically true with regards to the architecture of the temple, the doctrines of the temple, the symbolic stories of the endowment, and especially the ordinances of the temple itself—all these things combine to serve the purpose of orienting ourselves toward Christ and His infinite Atonement. In this chapter, we look at the clothing of the temple, which likewise serves as a symbolic reminder of His sacrifice for man and the powerful privilege we have to take His power upon us.

Ancient Temple Clothing and Meanings

Before discussing the Atonement symbolism inherent in temple clothing, it should be noted that special coverings have been part of the temple service since ancient times.

And Aaron and his sons thou shalt bring unto the door of the tabernacle of the congregation, and shalt *wash them with water*.

And thou shalt *take the garments*, and put upon Aaron *the coat*, and *the robe of the ephod*, and the ephod, and the breastplate, and gird him with the *curious girdle* of the ephod:

And thou shalt put the *mitre upon his head*, and put the holy crown upon the mitre.

Then shalt thou *take the anointing oil, and pour it upon his head, and anoint him*.

And thou shalt bring his sons, and put coats upon them.

And thou shalt *gird them with girdles*, Aaron and his sons, and *put the bonnets* on them: and the priest's office shall be theirs for a perpetual statute: and thou shalt consecrate Aaron and his sons. (Exodus 29:4–9; emphasis added)

Anciently, clothing was viewed as having a symbolic purpose by demonstrating or portraying the presence of God and His Spirit in your personal life. To cover yourself physically was to be reminded of the spiritual protection and cover provided through divine blessings and heavenly assistance. Said Moses, "I beheld the heavens open, and I was clothed upon with glory" (Moses 7:3).

Paul vividly compares the wearing of specific pieces of military armor with various aspects of God's power and salvation that individuals should put on in their spiritual life:

Finally, my brethren, *be strong in the Lord, and in the power of his might*.

Put on *the whole armour of God*, that ye may be able to stand against the wiles of the devil. . . .

Wherefore *take unto you the whole armour of God*, that ye may be able to withstand in the evil day, and having done all, to stand.

Stand therefore, *having your loins girt about with truth*, and having on the *breastplate of righteousness*;

And your *feet shod with the preparation of the gospel of peace*;

Above all, taking the *shield of faith*, wherewith ye shall be able to quench all the fiery darts of the wicked.

And take *the helmet of salvation*, and the *sword of the Spirit*, which is the word of God. (Ephesians 6:10–17; emphasis added)

In the parable of the Prodigal Son, we find the repentant younger son returning home with the sole hope that he could at best be brought back into the presence of his father and family as a lowly "hired servant"

(Luke 15:19). Imagine this younger son's surprise when the father not only accepts him back, but dons on him a ring and a robe—both items symbolically suggesting that he has been fully reinstated into the family with all privileges. He is clothed with power and authority. His newly bestowed coverings suggest he has been redeemed and restored through a power greater than his own.

On the other hand, we see in the scriptures portrayals of individuals who are not so clothed, even naked, thus portraying a lack of the divine in their life, or at least portraying their sinful state and loss of the Spirit. In another memorable parable of Jesus, the good Samaritan, we learn of another man who goes down from Jerusalem to Jericho. He falls among thieves and is stripped of his raiment and left "half dead" (Luke 10:30). Latter-day Saint scholar John Welch spoke of how research into this parable has yielded a different interpretation, at least for the early Christian saints, than the applications we make in modern times by way of themes of charity and service. Welch surmised that "this parable's content is clearly practical and dramatic in its obvious meaning, but a time-honored Christian tradition also saw the parable as an impressive allegory of the Fall and Redemption of mankind."[1] Welch further asserts, "The roots of this allegorical interpretation reach deep into early Christianity. In the second century AD, Irenaeus in France and Clement of Alexandria both saw the good Samaritan as symbolizing Christ Himself saving the fallen victim, wounded with sin."[2] Speaking of the symbolism of having his clothes stripped and stolen, Welch taught:

> Early Christians sensed that Jesus spoke of something important here. Origen and Augustine saw the loss of the traveler's garment as a symbol for mankind's loss of immortality and incorruptibility. Chrysostom spoke of the loss of "his robe of immortality" or "robe of obedience." Ambrose spoke of the traveler being "stripped of the covering of spiritual grace which we [all] received [from God]."
>
> The attackers apparently wanted the traveler's clothing, for no mention is made of any wealth or commodities he might be carrying. For some reason, the robbers seem interested in his garment, something brought down from the holy place and something they envy and want to take away.[3]

All of these ancient scriptural teachings help provided a context in which we can more fully see and appreciate the symbolic pattern that is prevalent in the clothing that one encounters in the temple endowment.

In Ezekiel 16, a vivid and powerful concept is taught where God gives life to Israel through blood (verse 6): He covers her nakedness (Israel's sins; verses 7–8), He makes a covenant with her (verse 8), He washes her with water (verse 9), He anoints her with oil (verse 9), He clothes her in robes and other symbolic apparel (verses 10–11), and finally He puts a crown upon her head (verse 12; see also Ruth 3:3–15). Thus, clothing in ancient settings and particularly in scriptural context suggests an important parallel with putting on one's self the power of God.

It is interesting to note the meaning of the word *atonement* as used in the Old Testament. The Hebrew word is *kaphar*, which literally translated means "to cover over." What a powerful reminder when discussing the symbolic nature of clothing, especially temple clothing; the idea being that we are clothed, or covered, in and by the Savior's Atonement.

Coverings in the Garden of Eden

Having established the symbolic perspective of clothing, especially as it relates to redemption and the Savior's Atonement, we now turn our attention back to the symbolic teachings of the Garden of Eden. As we consider Adam and Eve, the Savior's Atonement, and modern temple clothing, serval fascinating concepts begin to appear. Keep in mind the symbolic meaning not just of clothing, but the lack thereof. After partaking of the forbidden fruit, we read the following from the Pearl of Great Price:

> And the eyes of them both were opened, and *they knew that they had been naked. And they sewed fig leaves together and made themselves aprons.*
>
> And they heard the voice of the Lord God, as they were walking in the garden, in the cool of the day; and Adam and his wife *went to hide themselves from the presence of the Lord* God amongst the trees of the garden. (Moses 4:13–14; emphasis added)

I cannot help but wonder if God must have chuckled a bit when he saw their leafy attire. After confronting Adam and Eve, the Lord then gives several items of instruction, relative to the way they are to live and conduct themselves as mortals. He then says, "Unto Adam, and also unto his wife, did *I, the Lord God, make coats of skins, and clothed them*" (Moses 4:27; emphasis added).

Notice that twice Adam and Eve tried to cover themselves—first with fig leaves, and second by hiding behind the trees of the garden. The phrase "they sewed fig leaves together" is intriguing, especially when we consider once again the symbolic idea of clothing and the Hebrew word for atonement, *kaphar*, meaning "to cover."

In essence, Adam and Eve discover their nakedness, or, in other words, we discover we are devoid of the Spirit and lacking God's presence in our lives. Their first response of covering themselves could suggest that sometimes as God's spirit children here on earth, we try to save ourselves; we try to do it all on our own. We try to cover or *kaphar* ourselves.

Likewise intriguing is Heavenly Father's response. He says that He, Himself, will make coats of skins for them and clothe them Himself. The idea is this: We do not save ourselves. Only God can do that for us.

Furthermore, the implication that "coats of skins" were used suggest that an animal was sacrificed. It is as though the Father says to Adam and Eve: "Let me clothe you . . . and we will do it the right way this time. We will arrange a sacrifice, even a sacrifice of mine Only Begotten Son, so that you can be covered properly, so that you can be truly saved. I will arrange for you a salvation that you can never purchase. I will send my Son who alone possesses the ability and the willingness to perfectly provide that which I can see you truly desire."

As we go through the temple, even the clothing we receive and are invited to wear should motivate us to reflect upon and remember the true and only source of our salvation.

Saved by the Savior's Righteousness

Now, keeping the preceding truths in mind, let us further consider the symbolic ideas of temple clothing and salvation. While instructing his son Jacob, Lehi makes this sublime doctrinal declaration: "Wherefore, thy soul shall be blessed, and thou shalt dwell safely with thy brother, Nephi; and thy days shall be spent in the service of thy God. Wherefore, *I know that thou art redeemed, because of the righteousness of thy Redeemer*; for thou hast beheld that in the fulness of time he cometh to bring salvation unto men" (2 Nephi 2:3; emphasis added). This is fascinating. Lehi could have said, "Jacob, I know you are redeemed because of your righteousness," but he didn't. No, Lehi knows the doctrine. We are not redeemed because of our righteousness, we are redeemed because of the Savior's righteousness. We don't *kaphar* or cover ourselves. We don't clothe ourselves. No, God must clothe and cover us.

Paul likewise teaches this truth: "Brethren, *my heart's desire and prayer to God for Israel is, that they might be saved. For I bear them record* that they have a zeal of God, but not according to knowledge. For *they being ignorant of God's righteousness, and going about to establish their own righteousness, have not submitted themselves unto the righteousness of God"* (Romans 10:1–3; emphasis added). No wonder the same Jacob, brother of Nephi, would later testify and declare that "we shall have a perfect knowledge of all our guilt, *and our uncleanness, and our nakedness*; and the righteous shall have a perfect knowledge of their enjoyment, and their righteousness, *being clothed with purity, yea, even with the robe of righteousness"* (2 Nephi 9:14; emphasis added). Yes, even the robe of the Savior's righteousness! Isaiah rejoiced, saying, "[God] hath clothed me with the garments of salvation, he hath covered me with the robe of righteousness" (Isaiah 61:10). Alma referred to "all the holy prophets, whose garments are cleansed and are spotless, pure and white" (Alma 5:24) through the blood of Jesus Christ and His infinite Atonement.

Modern prophets have clearly taught this truth that we do not save and redeem ourselves. Elder Quentin L. Cook declared, "We must always remember that *we do not save ourselves. We are liberated by the love, grace,* and atoning sacrifice of the Savior."[4] Similarly, President Dieter F. Uchtdorf taught, "We cannot earn our way into heaven. . . . Are we confident and comfortable in our good deeds, trusting in our own righteousness? . . . Salvation cannot be bought with the currency of obedience; it is purchased by the blood of the Son of God. Thinking that we can trade our good works for salvation is like buying a plane ticket and then supposing we own the airline. Or thinking that after paying rent for our home, we now hold title to the entire planet earth."[5] He then asks why we should be obedient if our works do not save us. His reply: "Our obedience to God's commandments comes as a natural outgrowth of our endless love and gratitude for the goodness of God."[6] Such a belief in the saving power of Christ is truly the mark of a Christian. As Elder Robert D. Hales testified, "What does it mean to be a Christian? . . . A Christian believes that *through the grace of God the Father and His Son, Jesus Christ, we can repent, forgive others, keep the commandments,* and inherit eternal life."[7]

Nephi, Laban, and Symbolic Clothing

The idea of finding power, authority, and redemption through the donning of symbolic clothing can enhance the respect and reverence that we have for temple clothing. It likewise can enhance the way we read certain scriptural narratives dealing with clothing. The Book of Mormon contains a well-known story, which can take on a new and powerful meaning if we are willing to "liken the scriptures" unto ourselves just a little (see 1 Nephi 19:23). Although what follows is more of an application, rather than a contextual interpretation, the principles flowing from this scriptural account can be profound. After failing several times to get the brass plates, Nephi leaves his brothers for another attempt:

> And I was led by the Spirit, not knowing beforehand the things which I should do.
>
> Nevertheless I went forth, and as I came near unto the house of Laban I beheld a man, and he had fallen to the earth before me, for *he was drunken with wine.*
>
> And when I came to him I found that it was Laban.
>
> And I beheld his sword. . . .
>
> And it came to pass that I was constrained by the Spirit that I should kill Laban; but I said in my heart: Never at any time have I shed the blood of man. And I shrunk and would that I might not slay him.
>
> And the Spirit said unto me again: Behold the Lord hath delivered him into thy hands. . . .
>
> And it came to pass that the Spirit said unto me again: Slay him, for the Lord hath delivered him into thy hands;
>
> Behold the Lord slayeth the wicked to bring forth his righteous purposes. *It is better that one man should perish than that a nation should dwindle and perish in unbelief.* (1 Nephi 4:6–13; emphasis added)

For the moment, the man Laban is our focus. We are told he "was drunken with wine." In section 133 of the Doctrine and Covenants, we learn that when the Savior comes to earth a second time, He will not be wearing white clothing (as is often depicted in LDS art work). Rather, He will come "down from God in heaven with dyed garments; yea, from the regions which are not known, clothed in his glorious apparel, traveling in the greatness of his strength. . . . And *the Lord shall be red in his apparel, and his garments like him that treadeth in the wine-vat*" (D&C 133:46, 48; emphasis added). The Lord will then say, "*I have trodden the wine-press alone,* and have brought judgment upon all people; and none were with me; And I have trampled them in my fury, and I did tread upon them in mine anger, and *their blood have I sprinkled upon my garments, and stained all my raiment*; for this was the day of vengeance which was in my heart" (D&C 133:50–51; emphasis added).

The reason the Savior will be wearing red at His Second Coming is symbolic. The staining of His garments red comes from treading the wine-vat. This is symbolic of Him taking our sins upon Himself; it is as though He is "drunken with wine."

At this point some readers might be shocked that I am comparing Laban to Christ. Before we go further, consider the following: often we have an incorrect view of what it means that the Savior took upon himself our sins. Christ is bearing our sins, or becoming them. As Paul once said, Christ has been "made . . . to be sin for us, who knew no sin; that we might be made the righteousness of God in him" (2 Corinthians 5:21). In other words, Christ imputes to us His righteousness, and He takes our sin. In essence, He became the great sinner—He became the bad guy, just like Laban. Perhaps this is the reason why the Spirit so completely and utterly withdraws from Christ on the cross and at Gethsemane.

When one has sin, and the Savior became sin for us, all our sins, the Spirit cannot be present with that individual. Oh what gratitude and reverence we owe to our Savior!

What occurs next in the Nephite record is stunning when considered in symbolic fashion. After killing Laban, Nephi then tells us: "I took *the garments of Laban* and *put them upon mine own body; yea, even every whit*; and I did *gird on his armor about my loins*. And after I had done this, *I went forth unto the treasury of Laban*. And as I went forth towards the treasury of Laban, behold, I saw the servant of Laban *who had the keys of the treasury*. And *I commanded him in the voice of Laban*, that he should go with me into the treasury" (1 Nephi 4:19–20; emphasis added). Nephi put on the garments of the one who became sin, or who was a representation of sin, so to speak. He goes to the treasury—he looked like Laban, he sounded like Laban, and the treasure became his.

Putting on the temple garments can remind us that we are putting on Christ and the saving powers of His Atonement. Had Christ not given His life for us, none of us could make it back to the presence of the Father, and we could not attain the heavenly treasure.

> Wherefore, it must needs be an infinite atonement—save it should be an infinite atonement this corruption could not put on incorruption. Wherefore, the first judgment which came upon man must needs have remained to an endless duration. And if so, this flesh must have laid down to rot and to crumble to its mother earth, to rise no more.

O the wisdom of God, his mercy and grace! For behold, if the flesh should rise no more our spirits must become subject to that angel who fell from before the presence of the Eternal God, and became the devil, to rise no more.

And our spirits must have become like unto him, and we become devils, angels to a devil, to be shut out from the presence of our God, and to remain with the father of lies, in misery, like unto himself; yea, to that being who beguiled our first parents, who transformeth himself nigh unto an angel of light, and stirreth up the children of men unto secret combinations of murder and all manner of secret works of darkness. (2 Nephi 9:7–9)

Truly we can see, with humility, love, and reverence, that it really "is better that one man should perish than that a nation should dwindle and perish in unbelief" (1 Nephi 4:13). No doubt, "Therefore have we not great reason to rejoice? Yea, we have reason to praise him forever, for he is the Most High God, and has loosed our brethren from the chains of hell" (Alma 26:13–14).

Women and the Wearing of the Veil

During the endowment, a veil is worn by female patrons, which likewise has profound Atonement symbolism. Unfortunately, some women do not see or understand this, and even may erroneously feel that they are being treated differently than the men.

Nothing could be further from the truth. To understand at least one level of symbolism inherent in the wearing of the veil (and its connection to the Atonement), it may be helpful to understand some of the writings of Paul. In his epistle to the Ephesians, Paul speaks of the sacred relationship of husband and wife, comparing it to the relationship between Christ and the Church.

> Wives, submit yourselves unto your own husbands, as unto the Lord.
> *For the husband is the head of the wife, even as Christ is the head of the church*: and he is the saviour of the body.
> Therefore as the church is subject unto Christ, so let the wives be to their own husbands in every thing.
> Husbands, love your wives, even as Christ also loved the church, and gave himself for it. (Ephesians 5:22–25; emphasis added)

To understand the veil motif, we must understand that Paul is comparing the man to Christ and the woman to the Church. In the temple endowment, we could say that the women there, in a limited respect, represent not just women, but the whole Church—men included! With this in mind, let us now examine another statement from Paul. In his second epistle to the Corinthian saints, Paul gives this interesting counsel with regards to the wearing of the veil:

> But if the ministration of death, written and engraven in stones, was glorious, so that the *children of Israel could not steadfastly behold the face of Moses for the glory of his countenance*; which glory was to be done away:
>
> How shall not the ministration of the spirit be rather glorious?
>
> For if the ministration of condemnation be glory, much more doth the ministration of righteousness exceed in glory.
>
> For even that which was made glorious had no glory in this respect, by reason of the glory that excelleth.
>
> For if that which is done away was glorious, much more that which remaineth is glorious.
>
> Seeing then that we have such hope, we use great plainness of speech:
>
> And not as *Moses, which put a veil over his face*, that the children of Israel could not steadfastly look to the end of that which is abolished:
>
> *But their minds were blinded: for until this day remaineth the same veil untaken away in the reading of the old testament; which veil is done away in Christ.*
>
> But even unto this day, when Moses is read, *the veil is upon their heart.*
>
> Nevertheless when it shall turn to the Lord, the veil shall be taken away. (2 Corinthians 3:7–16; emphasis added)

The idea here is similar to what we covered in one of the previous chapters regarding the veil of the temple, which represents the law of justice—a barrier that keeps us from seeing or beholding God. It is as though the wearing of the veil symbolically reminds all of us (not just women) that we are all veiled from entering God's presence, unless that veil is done away with by Christ. Only He can satisfy the demands of justice, thus allowing us to enter back into the Father's presence. Interestingly, in a non-LDS wedding ceremony (if and when a wedding veil is used) it is the man, not the woman, that lifts the veil off the face. So it is that Christ, the bridegroom, is the one who removes the veil (the law of justice) so that all of us, if we so choose, can gain access to Heavenly Father's presence once again.

One Christian scholar made this observation: "Not only does the bridal veil show the modesty and purity of the bride and her reverence for God, it reminds us of the temple veil which was torn in two when Christ died on the cross. The removing of the veil took away the separation between God and man, giving believers access into the very presence of God. Since Christian marriage is a picture of the union between Christ and the church, we see another reflection of this relationship in the removal of the bridal veil. Through marriage, the couple now has full access to one another."[8]

Noted Latter-day Saint scholar Alonzo Gaskill surmises that "the veiled face is not a statement about the spiritual ignorance of women. On the contrary, it is a statement about the spiritual blindness of all mankind, including those in the Church—covenant Israel. . . . Thus, in antiquity when the woman clothed herself in a veil, in part, that act symbolized her acknowledgment that the Church (or covenant Israel) did not see clearly, and therefore needed its God . . . to guide the members of the Church safely home. Submission of the will to the bridegroom was the only way that this safe return could be accomplished—and the veil was a frank acknowledgement of that fact."[9]

The Doctrine and Covenants is replete with veil symbolism. Notice how each reference below deals with the spiritual blindness that we face on earth, both men and women, which can only be removed by Christ, the bridegroom: "the veil of darkness shall soon be rent" (D&C 38:8); "the veil shall be rent and you shall see me" (D&C 67:10); "the veil of the covering of my temple . . . shall be taken off" (D&C 101:23); "the veil was taken from our minds" (D&C 110:1). In none of these instances, nor in the Bible, is there exclusive mention of the veil being an article of clothing that is designated for women only. No, it is a symbol that represents the impeding cover (law of justice) that needs to be and can be removed from all of us but only through Jesus Christ's infinite Atonement.

Conclusion

Hopefully, as we have discussed the symbolism of the temple clothing, relative to the Atonement of Jesus Christ, there will come a positive, lasting change in how we regard this sacred clothing. In recent years, the Church has made great efforts to instruct the Saints and the world with regards to the sacred and reverential nature of temple clothing. Articles have been written, classes have been taught, even a new video clip on temple clothing has been released showing the robes of the Holy Priesthood—all this in an effort to help us and others cultivate an appropriate and sacred regard for these highly symbolic vestments. The choice is ours as to whether we will acquiesce to this invitation, or whether we will proceed nonchalantly with such sacred and serious symbolism at stake.

> I believe there is a critical body of knowledge relating to the temple garment," said Elder Carlos E. Asay, "When that knowledge is obtained, Latter-day Saints filled with faith wear the garment and wear it properly, not because someone is policing their actions but because they understand the virtues of the sacred clothing and want to 'do good and be restored unto that which is good.' On the other hand, when one does not understand the sacred nature of the temple garment, the tendency is to treat it casually and regard it as just another piece of cloth.[10]

In a letter to priesthood leaders dated October 10, 1988, the First Presidency made the following important statements regarding how the garment should be worn:

> Church members who have been clothed with the garment in the temple have made a covenant to wear it throughout their lives. This has been interpreted to mean that it is worn as underclothing both day and night. This sacred covenant is between the member and the Lord. Members should seek the guidance of the Holy Spirit to answer for themselves any personal questions about the wearing of the garment. . . . The promise of protection and blessings is conditioned upon worthiness and faithfulness in keeping the covenant.
>
> The fundamental principle ought to be to wear the garment and not to find occasions to remove it. Thus, members should not remove either all or part of the garment to work in the yard or to lounge around the home in swimwear or immodest clothing. Nor should they remove it to participate in recreational activities that can reasonably be done with the garment worn properly beneath regular clothing. When the garment must be removed, such as for swimming, it should be restored as soon as possible.
>
> The principles of modesty and keeping the body appropriately covered are implicit in the covenant and should govern the nature of all clothing worn. Endowed members of the Church wear the garment as a reminder of the sacred covenants they have made with the Lord and also as a protection against temptation and evil. How it is worn is an outward expression of an inward commitment to follow the Savior.[11]

May we treat temple clothing with respect and reverence, and may we wear it always and never find inappropriate occasion to remove it. And most importantly, may we thus be symbolically reminded to never find occasion to remove Christ and His Atonement from our lives. Let us "awake [and] put on the armor of righteousness" (2 Nephi 1:23); let us put on the Atonement of Christ.

Notes

1. John W. Welch, "The Good Samaritan: Forgotten Symbols," *Ensign*, February 2007, 41–42.
2. Ibid, 42.
3. Ibid, 43.
4. Quentin L. Cook, "Lamentations of Jeremiah: Beware of Bondage," *Ensign*, November 2013, 91; emphasis added.
5. Dieter F. Uchtdorf, "The Gift of Grace," *Ensign*, May 2015, 108–09.
6. Ibid, 109.
7. Robert D. Hales, "Being a More Christian Christian," *Ensign*, November 2012, 90; emphasis added.
8. Mary Fairchild, "Christian Wedding Customs and Traditions," ThoughtCo., last modified August 16, 2016, accessed May 16, 2017, http://christianity.about.com/od /weddingceremony/a/weddingtraditions_2.htm.
9. Alonzo Gaskill, *Sacred Symbols: Finding Meaning in Rites, Rituals, and Ordinances* (Springville, UT: Bonneville Books, 2011), 152–53.
10. Carlos E. Asay, "The Temple Garment," *Ensign*, August 1997.
11. First Presidency letter, October 10, 1988; as appears in Carlos E. Asay, "The Temple Garment," *Ensign*, August 1997.

Seven

Our Destiny:
Becoming Kings and Queens

*Remember that that which cometh from above is sacred, and must
be spoken with care, and by constraint of the Spirit; and in
this there is no condemnation. (D&C 63:64)*

*Why speakest thou unto them in parables? He answered and said unto
them, because it is given unto you to know the mysteries of the kingdom
of heaven, but to them it is not given. . . . Therefore speak I to them in
parables: because they seeing see not; and hearing they hear not, neither
do they understand. . . . But blessed are your eyes, for they see: and
your ears, for they hear. (Matthew 13:10–11, 13, 16)*

The temple is a place of holiness. It is a place of introspective instruction and light-filled learning. It is a timeless tutorial that uses sacred
symbols, often and overtly, to point God's children to their potential and
perpetual destiny. These symbols not only reveal God's doctrine, they
conceal it as well. John the Revelator once spoke somewhat cryptically
of our eternal potential as follows: "To him that overcometh will I grant
to sit with me in *my throne*, even as I also overcame, and am set down
with my *Father in his throne*. He that hath an ear, let him hear what
the Spirit saith" (Revelation 3:21–22; emphasis added). The notion of
obtaining a throne, of being crowned, of becoming kings and queens
is central to the theology and symbolism of God's holy house. In fact,
these regnal references not only denote salvation but are directly symbolic

of eternal life which is exaltation in the highest degree of heaven in the celestial glory.

Elder Bruce R. McConkie once commented on the symbolism of being crowned: "Those who gain exaltation in the highest heaven of the celestial world *shall wear crowns*. Perhaps literal crowns may be worn on occasion—emblematic of their victory over the world and signifying that *they rule and reign as kings and queens in the eternal house of Israel*."[1] Whether those crowns are literal remains to be seen in some future day. Regardless, the Lord has revealed the figurative nature of these crowns: "If ye are faithful ye shall be laden with many sheaves, and *crowned with honor, and glory, and immortality, and eternal life*" (D&C 75:5; emphasis added). This noble ideal is not only central to the temple, but to the very essence of Heavenly Father's eternal plan.

President Spencer W. Kimball once said: "We do not rear children just to please our vanity. We bring children into the world *to become kings and queens, priests and priestesses for our Lord*."[2] Lorenzo Snow once pleaded with the Saints to "conduct [themselves] with prudence in all things, and labor for the interests of the kingdom of God, and that we may not be among the foolish virgins, but be found worthy to be amongst those who will be crowned as *kings and queens and reign throughout eternity*."[3] Such individuals receive "eternal increase" (D&C 131); they receive "all power" and the "continuation of the seeds" (D&C 132); they receive the "father's kingdom" and "all that the Father hath" (D&C 84:33–38); they are filled "with His glory" and are "made equal with Him" (D&C 88:107); they become "joint heirs" with Christ (Romans 8:17); and they "sit in His throne" (Revelation 3:21). In short, they become gods and goddesses, kings and queens. This is the meaning and scope of all royal references in the scriptures.

The idea of becoming a king or queen, in a symbolic, spiritual, or eternal sense is intriguing. The notion that the faithful "shall inherit thrones, kingdoms, principalities, and powers, dominions, all heights and depths" (D&C 132:19) is entrancing and enthralling. There is an allure of sorts that we feel—an attraction to this lofty aspiration. There even seems to be with many in the world today and throughout history a fascination with royalty and regalia, with kingdoms and crowns, with princes and princesses. Whether it's through the tabloid news or fairy tales of old, the concept of hereditary nobility captures the imagination and inspires a longing to "live happily ever after." It is thus intriguing to consider that the Lord has commanded His children to not only obtain instruction "in principle, in doctrine, in the law of the gospel, [and] in all things that pertain unto the kingdom of God," but also instruction regarding "the wars and the perplexities of the nations, and the judgments which are on the land; and *a knowledge also of countries and of kingdoms*" (D&C 88:78–79; emphasis added).

Likewise, the Lord has declared: "verily I say unto you, that it is my will that you should hasten to translate my scriptures, and *to obtain a knowledge of history, and of countries, and of kingdoms*, of laws of God and man, *and all this for the salvation of Zion*" (D&C 93:53; emphasis added).

Why would the Lord want us to have knowledge of earthly kingdoms? It should be noted that the Church of Jesus Christ of Latter-day Saints doesn't claim to be a *new* religion, but a *restored* religion—a religion that once had anciently in its fulness from the foundation of the world (see D&C 128:18). Such a reality, because of multiple periods of apostasy, would naturally leave a trail of theological debris in other altered (or otherwise corrupted) religious and philosophical systems throughout the history of mankind. Perhaps the Lord wants us to study these earthly kingdoms and systems not just so we will avoid the mistakes of history, but perhaps to enlighten and instruct us as well. Perhaps He wants us to unlock the symbols of our own sacred theology through the preserved, albeit tainted, allegories of antiquity. Although we cannot discuss specific details of certain aspects of the temple endowment ceremony due to their sacred nature, we can draw parallels between the endowment and the coronation ceremony of monarchs. By so doing we will hopefully better understand and appreciate the beauty, purpose, and symbolic meaning of this sacred ordinance.

Coronation of Kings and Queens

Various countries and peoples have established and enacted coronation ceremonies over the centuries past in order to distinguish and proclaim the reign of earthly kings and queens. Interestingly, many of these ceremonies claim precedence from the holy scriptures. The form of coronation between cultures and countries is very similar, as should be expected, since many of these ceremonies once had a common source. The following is a basic summary of the most common elements of the coronation of kings and queens. As you gain "a knowledge also of countries and of kingdoms" herein, it is hoped that your ears will indeed hear and that your eyes will be opened. Furthermore, it is hoped that you will be able to relate to this statement made by Joseph Smith, as it applies to the holy temples and their associated system of gospel instruction: "Our minds being now enlightened, we began to have the scriptures laid open to our understandings, and the true meaning and intention of their more mysterious passages revealed unto us in a manner which we never could attain to previously, nor ever before had thought of" (Joseph Smith—History 1:74).

Procession of Guests into Sacred Rooms or Edifices

Coronation and other enthronement rites often begin with processions (or marches) which can include the entrance of royalty, heads of state, and other invited guests into the chapels, halls, cathedrals, or sacred rooms that are prepared for the coronation ceremonies. Sacred music often accompanies this initial stage of the service, including the singing of anthems, which often are based on scriptural or liturgical texts. An example from the British coronation is the singing of the anthem from Psalm 122:1, which includes the phrase: "I was glad when they said unto me, let us go into the house of the Lord." Such anthems and music help contribute to the ambiance and aesthetic atmosphere that is desired to prepare the invited guests for the occasion at hand.

Coronation of Emperor Nicholas II of Russia and Empress Alexandra
Feodorovna in 1896. The king and queen at the altar, the men
of the court to the right, and the women to the left in veils.
Painting by Laurits Tuxen (1853–1927)

Receiving a New Name

Kings, queens, popes, and other sovereigns commonly receive a new name when they ascend to the throne or are elected to office. Often this new name is referred to as the *regnal* or *reign name*. For popes it is referred to as the papal name. In ancient Egypt pharaohs received a throne name as opposed to the temple name, as it is often referred to in East Asia. This new name is scripturally, genealogically, hereditarily, or historically based and is given and used so as to remind the monarchs and those they serve of their change in title, status, and function as empowered servants to benefit their subordinates. The practice of giving a new name dates back to ancient times and has occurred even with laity or nonroyal members of religious congregations, often referred to as one's religious name or spiritual name.

Washings and Anointing

Washings and anointings are often performed in the beginning of the coronation ceremony. This part of the coronation or enthronement rite claims ancient roots dating back to biblical times.

> And Aaron and his sons thou shalt bring unto the door of the tabernacle of the congregation, and *shalt wash them with water.*
>
> And thou shalt take the garments, and put upon Aaron the coat, and the robe of the ephod, and the ephod, and the breastplate, and gird him with the curious girdle of the ephod:
>
> And thou shalt put the mitre upon his head, and put the holy crown upon the mitre.
>
> Then shalt thou *take the anointing oil, and pour it upon his head, and anoint him.*
>
> And thou shalt bring his sons, and put coats upon them.
>
> And thou shalt gird them with girdles, Aaron and his sons, and put the bonnets on them: and the priest's office shall be theirs for a perpetual statute: and thou shalt consecrate Aaron and his sons. (Exodus 29:4–9; emphasis added)

When Queen Elizabeth II ascended to the British throne in 1952, a prayer was uttered by the archbishop that included these words: "O Lord and heavenly Father, the exalter of the humble and the strength of thy chosen, who by anointing with Oil didst of old make and consecrate kings, priests, and prophets, to teach and govern thy people Israel: Bless and sanctify thy chosen servant . . . who by our office and ministry is now to be anointed with this Oil. . . . Strengthen her, O Lord, with the

Holy Ghost the Comforter; Confirm and establish her with thy free and princely Spirit."⁴ At this point in the ceremony, Elizabeth sat down in King Edward's Chair to be anointed. The dean of Westminster poured some holy oil into the filigreed spoon, and with it the archbishop anointed the queen's head, palms, and breast with holy oil. And finally the crown of the head includes these words of dedication, "Be thy Head anointed with holy Oil: as kings, priests, and prophets were anointed: . . . you may at last be made partaker of an eternal kingdom, through the same Jesus Christ our Lord. Amen."⁵

While the British coronation ceremony involves anointing three places (head, palms, and breast), the French coronation has five places of anointing. In this case, the French monarch removes all clothing except for a long shirt and stands barefoot to receive the anointing on the hands, within the breast, between the shoulders, and in the break of the arm (the elbow) and on the head in the manner of a cross with the holy oil.

Alonzo Gaskill surmises that "the washing with water cleansed the initiate, and prepared him or her to receive the Holy Spirit, which was typically symbolized among the ancients by the act of anointing with oil from a horn."⁶ The acts of washing and then anointing can be seen as symbols of Christ, "whose title means quite literally 'anointed one.' Hence, to be washed led to an anointing, and to be anointed suggested that one was God's representative. The rite was, in the very least, a commitment on the part of the initiate to live and minister as God would."⁷ To be covered so completely in oil serves as a reminder that "it is only in and through the grace of God that [we] are saved" (2 Nephi 10:24).

Royalty, in the ancient, worldly setting, was something that was usually inherited and not earned or purchased. Thus it is that becoming a king or a queen, in a spiritual or eternal sense, is an honor that is not merited or earned—it is a right bestowed through the mercy and grace of Christ to those who are accepting of Him, whose crown it is, to give to those willing to receive. Enoch readily understood this truth: "thou hast made me, *and given unto me a right to thy throne*, and not of myself, *but through thine own grace*" (Moses 7:59; emphasis added).

Preliminary Clothing in Plain White Garments

After the washing and anointing portion of the enthronement or coronation ceremony, the monarch receives and is clothed in a simple white linen undergarment called the *colobium sindonis*. This unadorned garment symbolizes divesting oneself of vanity, eschewing all things worldly, and standing bare before God. During the Coronation of Elizabeth II, the queen sat down in King Edward's Chair, whereupon the dean of Westminster, assisted by a female attendant, put upon her the *colobium sindonis* (Latin for "shroud tunic"). The queen then received further clothing, all preliminary to the final clothing in royal robes.

Kneeling before the Altar / Taking of Oaths and Promises
At this point, the monarch is brought before the altar where upon is placed a Bible (or other holy texts) and often other various items of familial significance. Solemn oaths are taken and entered into, often prefaced with the following phrase as the charge is given to the royal initiate: "Will you solemnly promise and swear to . . ." and "Will you to the utmost of your power maintain the Laws of God and the true profession of the gospel?"[8] The charges and oaths administered and entered into are numerous and sacred, often involving commitment to God's laws, service to one's fellow beings, and one's own self comportment.

Clothing in Royal Robes
The monarch receives royal robes, which, depending on the point in the ceremony, are often placed on a particular shoulder; sometimes being switched later in the ceremony to the other shoulder. During the coronation of Elizabeth II, the words of instruction were given by the archbishop: "Receive this Imperial Robe, and the Lord God endue [endow] you with knowledge and wisdom, with majesty and power from on high; *the Lord clothe you with the robe of righteousness, and with the garments of salvation.* Amen."[9] The symbolism here is straightforward and intriguing. The language, parsed from Isaiah, indicates a "robe of righteousness"— perhaps serving as a reminder to the royal initiate that righteousness is not a function of an internal production or effort, but rather as a reception of an external source.

Receiving and Holding Various Items of Regalia
During a coronation, various items of regalia are given to and received by the monarch. Typical items include an orb, the sword of state, the royal ring (signet ring), the scepter, and a crown. The sword of state (also known as the sword of justice or mercy), is one of the first items received and is sometimes lifted and held forward in the right hand, with the right arm to the square. In other ceremonies, depending on the nation, the sword is held with two hands and represents the power of a monarch to defend his or her country against their enemies. It also symbolizes ultimate

jurisdictional power. The orb, usually surmounted with a cross, typifies Christ's reign over the earth, thus symbolizing the bestowal and reception of celestial reward (e.g., "the meek shall inherit the earth"—see Matthew 5:5). The orb is received by the monarch by placing the cupped hand underneath the orb. At the beginning of the coronation ceremony, the orb is delivered into the monarch's right hand. The orb is then placed on the altar where it remains until the end of the ceremony. At the conclusion, the monarch holds the orb in the left hand, while holding the scepter in the right hand. The ring is a symbol of the authority and power of the monarch and is received by placing the right hand forward with the palm turned down. The archbishop places the ring on the fourth finger of the monarch's right hand.

First-century statue of Jupiter in the Hermitage (left), with robe on the left shoulder, holding the scepter in the left hand with arm to the square, and the right hand in cupping shape underneath the orb. Other kings and emperors (i.e., roman emperor to the right) receive various items of regalia in similar fashion.

Crowning of the Monarch

The culminating act of the enthronement or coronation ceremony is the reception of the crown. In the British coronation, the archbishop holds the crown with both hands, high above the head of the monarch, then places the crown on the monarch while the congregation exults in a united voice three times: "God save the King! God save the King! God save the King!" The congregation immediately follows the crowning of the monarch by placing coronets and caps on their heads. In some enthronement ceremonies, the monarch receives the crown with both hands outstretched, high above their head, lowering the crown three times on their head. Often in coronation and enthronement ceremonies, this scripture in Psalms is recited as follows: "Let my prayer come up into thy presence as the incense: and let *the lifting up of my hands be as an evening sacrifice.* Alleluia" (Psalm 141:2; emphasis added).

Queen Elizabeth II holding the scepter and the orb at her coronation in 1953

Conclusion

It is interesting to note that during a relatively short period of time during the Middle Ages, some European kings elected to have their heirs apparent anointed and crowned during their own lifetime in order to avoid succession disputes. This practice was seen in England, France, and also Hungary, to name a few places. These heirs didn't become royalty in the moment of the coronation, yet they were anointed and crowned to become such one day, depending on their faithfulness in fulfilling the vows of office and living to fulfill their destined vocation. These junior kings (*rex iunior*), had very little authority and could not exercise the full power of office until the day came when they actually ascended to the throne as the reigning monarchs of their nations.

So it is that when we are endowed, we are not just washed and anointed *as* kings and queens, but to *become such one day!* The fulfilling of this reality likewise depends on our faithfulness in keeping our covenants and promises.

In an earlier chapter, we discussed the four pillars of eternity: the Creation, the Fall, the Atonement, and exaltation. It could be said that these four doctrines are not only the core doctrines taught in the temple endowment, but they form the basis around which temple symbols are constructed as well. In fact, most if not all symbols of the temple deal with one of two things: (1) Christ and His Atonement, or (2) the outcomes of His Atonement—even eternal life and exaltation! Every place we sit, every action we make, everything we see and say—all of it combined in one way or another symbolically points us to one of these two realities. Thus, a better understanding of the coronation ceremony can help us appreciate and better understand this second component, mainly, our belief and desire as Latter-day Saints to one day become exalted, to become *"kings and queens, priests and priestesses for our Lord,"*[10] which can only come through the infinite Atonement of our Lord Jesus Christ.

To Thy Throne We'll Come

C. Robert Line

Come and wash us, oh Jehovah, Zion's King, with water pure.
Cleanse our stains; pronounce us holy. Ancient promises assure!
Cover us with oil unblemished, as thy blood did freely flow—
Head and arms and back to strengthen, eyes and ears thy Truth to know.

Clothe us with the Spirit Holy; Robes of Righteousness bestow.
Gird us now with life eternal, seeds forevermore to sow.
Royal sons and daughters make us who before thy throne do bow.
Swords of truth we'll raise before us, in remembrance of our vow.

Lord, dost Thou the earth now grant us—orbs celestial, promised lands?
Scepter of divine dominion wilt Thou place in outstretched hands?
Ring of power, ring eternal? Gifts of mercy, gifts of grace!
Grateful hands we reach to heaven; in truth's round we seek Thy face.

Thou hast covered us completely; Thou the prize hast won alone.
Thou prepar'dst the Way before for us to sit with Thee on Thy throne.
Come, bestow thy crown, Jehovah! Thrice we raise our voice to Thee!
To Thy throne we'll come most boldly throughout all eternity!

Notes

1. Bruce R. McConkie, *Mormon Doctrine*, 2nd ed. (Salt Lake City: Deseret Book, 1966), 173; emphasis added.
2. Spencer W. Kimball, "Train Up a Child," *Ensign*, April 1978; emphasis added.
3. Lorenzo Snow, *Teachings of Presidents of the Church: Lorenzo Snow* (2011), 283; emphasis added.
4. Bryce Haymond, "U.K. Coronation Ceremony as an Endowment," Temple Study, last modified April 10, 2008, accessed May 17, 2017, http://www.templestudy .com/2008/04/10/coronation-ceremonyof-queen-elizabeth-ii.
5. "1953. The Coronation of Queen Elizabeth II: 'The Holy Anointing,'" YouTube video, 2:09, from the coronation of Queen Elizabeth II on June 2, 1953, posted by "pedrcymro29," October 21, 2013, https://www.youtube.com/watch ?v=ZYay408Rd7c.
6. Alonzo Gaskill, *Sacred Symbols: Finding Meaning in Rites, Rituals, and Ordinances* (Springville, UT: Bonneville Books, 2011), 40.
7. Ibid.
8. "English Coronation Oath," *Conservapedia*, last modified February 5, 2012, accessed May 17, 2017, http://www.conservapedia.com/English_coronation_oath.
9. Bryce Haymond, "U.K. Coronation Ceremony as an Endowment," Temple Study, last modified April 10, 2008, accessed May 17, 2017, http://www.templestudy .com/2008/04/10/coronation-ceremonyof-queen-elizabeth-ii; emphasis added; see Isaiah 61:10.
10. Spencer W. Kimball, "Train Up a Child," *Ensign*, April 1978; emphasis added.

Eight

Growing in the Light
of the Temple

That which is of God is light; and he that receiveth light, and continueth
in God, receiveth more light; and that light groweth brighter and
brighter until the perfect day. (D&C 50:24)

The night is far spent, the day is at hand: let us therefore cast off the works
of darkness, and let us put on the armour of light. (Romans 13:12)

The temple is a place of light.[1] This is clearly seen in the architecture, illumination, and pedagogy of this sacred edifice. Temples are often bathed in a glorious glow amidst the darkness of the night. In the temple it is as though one is surrounded by light. Whether it be reflecting mirrors, brightly lit open spaces, or beautiful décor, there is a feeling that one is immersed in light. This is by design and thus serves as a powerful symbol of the spiritual light we can and do receive. To enter the temple is to enter the light. As we are illuminated by the light of the temple, we change and so does our view of the world around us. C. S. Lewis once observed: "I believe in Christianity as I believe that the sun has risen: not only because I see it, but because by it I see everything else."[2]

Such is the case with the temples of the Lord. We are given new perspectives through which we begin to properly discern the true nature of our existence here on earth and into the eternities. Temples serve as patterns through which we can grow increasingly in the light. "And if your eye be single to my glory, your whole bodies shall be filled with light, and there shall be no darkness in you; and that body which is filled with light comprehendeth all things" (D&C 88:67). In the temple we are invited to "walk in the light of the Lord" (2 Nephi 12:5) that we may become "the children of light" (John 12:36). We are instructed in the temple to clothe ourselves in symbolic robes, which can remind us that the Lord really wants us to "put on the armour of light" (Romans 13:12). We are commanded from the "Father of lights" (James 1:17) to "bring up [our] children in light and truth" (D&C 93:40). "This then is the message which we have heard of him, and declare unto you, that God is light, and in him is no darkness at all" (1 John 1:5). In this chapter we discuss the concept of spiritual light as it relates to temples.

Patterns of Light

Light varies in brightness and intensity. Astronomers are fond of reminding us of our statistically favored, fortunate, and unusual existence here on this bright blue planet in a region of our solar system they call the *Goldilocks zone*—this is to say that if we were any closer to the sun things would be "too hot," and we would burn up. Any further away from the sun and things are "too cold," and we would freeze. No, things here on earth are "just right," and life exists in abundance.

Spiritual light also varies in brightness and intensity, and we must stay in the proper "zone" to maintain and grow in our spiritual life. Too much spiritual light can be counterproductive and even damning in a sense. Too little light and our testimonies freeze over and diminish.

> And therefore, he that will harden his heart, the same receiveth the lesser portion of the word; and he that will not harden his heart, *to him is given the greater portion of the word, until it is given unto him to know the mysteries of God until he know them in full.*
>
> And *they that will harden their hearts, to them is given the lesser portion of the word until they know nothing* concerning his mysteries; and then they are taken captive by the devil, and led by his will down to destruction. Now this is what is meant by the chains of hell. (Alma 12:10–11; emphasis added)

Having the proper balance of spiritual light in our life is critical, but we must always remember the Master's injunction: "Behold, ye are little children and *ye cannot bear all things now*; ye must grow in grace and in the knowledge of the truth" (D&C 50:40; emphasis added). No, we need to stay in our spiritual Goldilocks zone if we are to continue our path toward life eternal.

A pattern is found in the Savior's instruction to the Nephites that we can and should apply to the light and knowledge we can continually receive in the temple: "I perceive that ye are weak, that *ye cannot understand all my words* which I am commanded of the Father to speak unto you at this time. Therefore, *go ye unto your homes*, and *ponder upon the things which I have said*, and ask of the Father, in my name, that ye may understand, and *prepare your minds for the morrow, and I come unto you again*" (3 Nephi 17:2–3; emphasis added). We are given truth and light "line upon line, precept upon precept, here a little and there a little; and blessed are those who hearken unto my precepts, and lend an ear unto my counsel, for they shall learn wisdom; for *unto him that receiveth I will give more*; and *from them that shall say, We have enough, from them shall be taken away* even that which they have" (2 Nephi 28:30; emphasis added).

Obedience is the key to spiritual growth. Receiving more light is possible, and we can expand our spiritual Goldilocks zone, but growing in spiritual light is not a function of intellectual effort alone. No, it is a function of our willingness to follow and act on the light we already have. "It is given unto many to know the mysteries of God; nevertheless they are laid under a strict command that they shall not impart only according to the portion of his word which he doth grant unto the children of men, *according to the heed and diligence which they give unto him*" (Alma 12:9; emphasis added). Elder Gene R. Cook wisely counseled: "If you become one who just knows the truths rather than one who seeks to apply them, you will not teach by the spirit and you will not change people's lives, including your own. The Lord gives us truth on the basis of how fast we apply them. If you'll put them into your life—changing self, repenting—the Lord will continue to give you more and more."[3]

Staying in the spiritual Goldilocks zone requires patience. Although we might wish to know all things all at once, we must realize that God works otherwise. We must strive to learn more and more, especially in the temple, but at the same time me must learn to be content with where we are while not being complacent—it is a fine balance. Nephi tells us repeatedly that he rejoices not in simplicity but in plainness! "For my soul delighteth in plainness; for after this manner doth the Lord God work among the children of men. For the Lord God giveth light unto the understanding; for he speaketh unto men according to their language, unto their understanding" (2 Nephi 31:3).

That which is plain is not necessarily simple. Take someone who understands calculus, as an example: for them calculus is plain—that is, they understand it. But no one in their right mind would classify calculus as simple. No, God speaks to us, even in the temple, in plainness; He speaks unto us "according to [our] language, [meaning] unto [our] understanding" (2 Nephi 31:3). The beauty of the instruction of the temple is it can meet us wherever we are in our spiritual understanding; whatever our spiritual Goldilocks zone is, we will be instructed therein. Elder Francis M. Lyman perceptively observed:

> The Gospel is suited to *all the conditions of mankind*. It will meet every requirement of man, and it will satisfy every rational ambition and every righteous desire of the human heart. It is perfect in every respect. It is broad enough and deep enough for the rich and for the poor, for the intelligent and for the ignorant. *It will bring to every person exactly what is necessary for his salvation.* If men need to be humbled, it will school them. If they need to be exalted, it will lift them up. If they have need to be reformed, it will reform them. In fact, as I have said, it will meet all the requirements of human nature.[4]

True it is then, that "He that keepeth his commandments receiveth truth and light, until he is glorified in truth and knoweth all things" (D&C 93:28). In Doctrine and Covenants 50:24, we are given a succinct summary of the process of growing in the light: "That which is of God is light; and he that receiveth light, and continueth in God, receiveth more light; and that light groweth brighter and brighter until the perfect day." The temple is and can be an integral part of this process of growing in the light. In the rest of this chapter, we will examine different terms that relate to growing in the light and how these terms further relate to the temple.

The Light of Christ

In the temple endowment, we see the portrayal, perhaps figuratively, of the very first step we take as mortals in growing in the light, namely, the Light of Christ. Adam and Eve learned that the partaking of the forbidden fruit was necessary, not just so that they could have children (see 2 Nephi 2:22–25), but also that by so doing their "eyes [would] be opened, and [they would] be as gods, *knowing good and evil.* And when the woman saw that the tree was good for food, and that it became pleasant to the eyes, and a tree to be desired to make her wise, she took of the fruit thereof, and did eat, and also gave unto her husband with her, and he did eat. And the eyes of them both were opened" (Moses 4:11–13; emphasis added).

Our Father in Heaven said to His "Only Begotten: Behold, the man is become as one of us to know good and evil" (Moses 4:28). The Light of Christ, sometimes called the Spirit of Christ, is "given to every man, that he may know [or see or distinguish] good from evil" (Moroni 7:16). Some might refer to this as our conscience. We are told by the Lord that this light is "the light which shineth, which giveth you light, [and] is through him who enlighteneth your eyes, which is the same light that quickeneth your understandings" (D&C 88:11). In the Book of Mormon, we learn that all "men are instructed sufficiently that they know good from evil" (2 Nephi 2:5).

In addition to this rudimentary discerning function, the Light of Christ also plays another important role in our spiritual growth in the light. President Joseph F. Smith taught: "It is the Spirit of [Christ] that enlightens every man that comes into the world, and that strives with the children of men, and will continue to strive with them, until it brings them to a knowledge of the truth and the possession of the *greater light and testimony of the Holy Ghost*."[5]

The Power of the Holy Ghost

As you continue to grow in the light, you are thus led through the Light of Christ to a greater endowment of light, even the Holy Ghost. It should be understood, however, that the "Holy Ghost is manifested to men and women on the earth *both as the power and as the gift of the Holy Ghost*. The power can come upon a person before baptism; it is the convincing witness that Jesus Christ is our Savior and Redeemer. Through the power of the Holy Ghost, sincere investigators can acquire a conviction of the truthfulness of the Savior's gospel, of the Book of Mormon, of the reality of the Restoration, and of the prophetic calling of Joseph Smith."[6] No doubt Adam and Eve advanced from a reliance on the Light of Christ to the influence of the power of the Holy Ghost, which serves the primary function of confirming gospel truths as previously stated.

In the endowment, one learns that Adam and Eve receive the "convincing witness" that they are being taught by true messengers. Although they would later receive the gift of the Holy Ghost, they had fundamental truths confirmed to them by the power of the Holy Ghost.

Gift of the Holy Ghost

The gift of the Holy Ghost is an even greater endowment of light than the power of the Holy Ghost. The gift of the Holy Ghost though comes through an ordinance, and it entitles the recipient to comfort, peace, and guidance beyond what the individual not so endowed is entitled to receive. Although we perform this ordinance vicariously for the deceased in the temple, the endowment is silent on Adam and Eve receiving the gift of the Holy Ghost. However, we learn from the Pearl of Great Price that it was nonetheless received:

> And it came to pass, when the Lord had spoken with Adam, our father, that Adam cried unto the Lord, and he was caught away by the Spirit of the Lord, and was carried down into the water, and was laid under the water, and was brought forth out of the water.
>
> And thus he was baptized, and the *Spirit of God descended upon him, and thus he was born of the Spirit, and became quickened in the inner man.*
>
> And he heard a voice out of heaven, saying: Thou art baptized with fire, *and with the Holy Ghost.* This is the record of the Father, and the Son, from henceforth and forever. (Moses 6:64–66; emphasis added)

Baptism by Fire

After the power of the Holy Ghost and the gift of the Holy Ghost are received, there is another step that can be taken to grow further in the light. The temple, it seems, is perfectly designed to help us take this next step. To introduce this higher step of light, we turn to the words of Nephi:

> Wherefore, my beloved brethren, I know that if ye shall follow the Son, with full purpose of heart, acting no hypocrisy and no deception before God, but with real intent, repenting of your sins, witnessing unto the Father that ye are willing to take upon you the name of Christ, by baptism—yea, by following your Lord and your Savior down into the water, according to his word, behold, *then shall ye receive the Holy Ghost; yea, then cometh the baptism of fire and of the Holy Ghost;* and then can ye speak with the tongue of angels, and shout praises unto the Holy One of Israel. (2 Nephi 31:13; emphasis added)

Here we see an interesting punctuation with the use of a semicolon, which has doctrinal ramifications. Nephi clearly distinguishes between "the Holy Ghost" and "then cometh the baptism of fire," which is an even greater endowment of light. It could well be that there are some (if not many) members of the Church who are baptized and confirmed members, but have they experienced the baptism of fire through the Holy Ghost? Although we might use these terms as synonyms on occasion, there is nonetheless an important distinction that needs to be made. Elder Bednar once said: "We are commanded and instructed to so live that our fallen nature is changed through the *sanctifying power* of the Holy Ghost. . . . The baptism of fire by the Holy Ghost 'converts [us] from carnality to spirituality. It cleanses, heals, and purifies the soul. . . . Faith in the Lord Jesus Christ, repentance, and water baptism are all preliminary and prerequisite to it, but *[the baptism of fire] is the consummation.*'"[7]

The sanctifying influence that we can receive through the baptism of fire is greatly enhanced through temple service and attendance. In the dedicatory prayer of the Kirtland Temple, which Joseph Smith received by revelation from the Lord, the plea is made on behalf of the Saints "that they may grow up in thee, and receive a *fulness of the Holy Ghost*, and be organized according to thy laws, and be prepared to obtain every needful thing" (D&C 109:15; emphasis added). It is one thing to receive the Holy Ghost, but another to receive the "fulness" of the Holy Ghost. In the dedicatory prayer of the Indianapolis Indiana Temple, the officiator supplicated the Father with these words: "Bless all with a feeling of Thy love, a spirit of consecration, and a desire to assist Thee in Thy great work of bringing immortality and eternal life unto Thy children of all generations. *May the sanctifying influence of this house be extended into the families, the neighborhoods, and the communities* of those who will come to this temple."[8] Through the temple, the light can indeed "groweth brighter and brighter" (D&C 50:24).

The Strait and Narrow Path and Enduring to the End

The next step to growing in the light can best be summarized, once again, by Nephi's words:

> Wherefore, do the things which I have told you I have seen that your Lord and your Redeemer should do; for, for this cause have they been shown unto me, that ye might know the gate by which ye should enter.

For the gate by which ye should enter is repentance and baptism by water; and *then cometh a remission of your sins by fire and by the Holy Ghost.*

And *then are ye in this strait and narrow path* which leads to eternal life. . . .

And now, my beloved brethren, after ye have gotten into this strait and narrow path, I would ask if all is done? Behold, I say unto you, Nay; for ye have not come thus far save it were by the word of Christ with unshaken faith in him, relying wholly upon the merits of him who is mighty to save.

Wherefore, ye must press forward with a steadfastness in Christ, having a perfect brightness of hope, and a love of God and of all men. Wherefore, if ye shall press forward, feasting upon the word of Christ, and *endure to the end,* behold, thus saith the Father: Ye shall have eternal life. (2 Nephi 31:17–20; emphasis added)

It is interesting to note that, according to Nephi, an individual isn't even on the path until the baptism of fire has begun. Then, once on the path, his admonition is to endure to the end. Enduring to the end is not just barely "hanging on" to the end; no, it is enduring *well.* It is continuing on the path in a born again state. Enduring is also inextricably linked to covenant keeping, especially those covenants we make in the House of the Lord. Stephen Robinson once explained:

Most frequently, the scriptures use the term *endure* to mean "to last," "to continue," or "to remain," rather than "to suffer." For example, Alma expresses hope that his son Shiblon "will *continue* in keeping [God's] commandments; for blessed is he that *endureth* to the end." (Alma 38:2.) Nephi explains that we must "be reconciled unto Christ, and enter into the narrow gate, and walk in the strait path which leads to life, and continue in the path until the end of the day of probation." (2 Ne. 33:9.) *Thus, to endure is to continue in the path we adopted at baptism by keeping our commitments to Christ, until the end of our mortal life.*

Usually the scriptures link "enduring to the end" with keeping one's covenants with Christ. (See, for example, D&C 20:29; 2 Ne. 9:24.)[9]

Calling and Election

After we have endured sufficiently, after we have passed the trials of this life and proven ourselves worthy, there is another step that can occur as we grow in the light. A step that is also directly linked to the temple. Another look at Nephi's words yields this subtle yet profound detail: "Wherefore, if ye shall press forward, feasting upon the word of Christ, and endure to the end, *behold, thus saith the Father: Ye shall have eternal life*" (2 Nephi 31:20; emphasis added). All this is to say that once we have endured sufficiently and done all that we came here to earth to do, we shall have eternal life. This promise or declaration is what is sometimes referred to as one's "calling and election"—or having one's calling and election made sure.

Elder Bruce R. McConkie explained: "To have one's calling and election made sure is to be sealed up unto eternal life; it is to have the unconditional guarantee of exaltation in the highest heaven of the celestial world; it is to receive the assurance of godhood; it is, in effect, to have the day of judgment advanced, so that an inheritance of all the glory and honor of the Father's kingdom is assured prior to the day when the faithful actually enter into the divine presence."[10] The calling and election has several synonyms: sometimes it is referred to as "the promise of eternal life," or "the promise of exaltation," or "the more sure word of prophesy."

Although some Church members are not always familiar with this term (and this aspect of growing in the light), it is interesting to note that it is mentioned frequently in scripture and even in two of our hymns.[11] In the fourth verse of hymn number 21, "Come, Listen to a Prophet's Voice," we encounter these lyrics:

> Then heed the words of truth and light
> That flow from fountains pure.
> Yea, keep His law with all thy might
> *Till thine election's sure,*
> Till thou shalt *hear the holy voice*
> *Assure eternal reign,*
> While joy and cheer attend thy choice,
> *As one who shall obtain.*[12]

Also we come across these lyrics from the fourth verse of hymn number 134, "I Believe in Christ":

> I believe in Christ; he stands supreme!
> From him I'll gain my fondest dream;
> And while I strive through grief and pain,
> *His voice is heard: "Ye shall obtain."*
> I believe in Christ; so come what may,
> With him I'll stand in that great day
> When on this earth he comes again
> To rule among the sons of men.[13]

Some might ask: So how does one make their calling and election sure? To be sure, there are many scriptures, as mentioned previously, that discuss this event. However, there are very few that explain how you can know when this has occurred in your life. There is this plain verse, though, from section 131 of the Doctrine and Covenants, that states: "The more sure word of prophecy [calling and election] means a man's knowing that he is sealed up unto eternal life, by [1] *revelation and the spirit of prophecy*, [and, 2] *through the power of the Holy Priesthood*" (D&C 131:5; emphasis added). These two aspects are worth noting. First, a person will know this has occurred through revelation from the Holy Ghost (again, spiritual light is involved). Second, there is priesthood power that is associated with this event, meaning of course, there is an ordinance involved, including and in extension to, the ordinance of celestial marriage in the temple. Elder Bruce R. McConkie said:

> Making one's *calling and election sure comes after and grows out of celestial marriage*. Eternal life does not and cannot exist for a man or a woman alone, because in its very nature it consists of the continuation of the family unit in eternity. Thus the revelation on marriage speaks both of celestial marriage (in which the conditional promises of eternal life are given) and of making one's calling and election sure (in which the unconditional promises of eternal life are given) in one and the same sentence—which sentence also says that those who commit sins (except "murder whereby to shed innocent blood") after being sealed up unto eternal life shall still gain exaltation. This is the language: "Then"—that is, after their calling and election has been made sure— [D&C 132:19–20 cited].
>
> Then the revelation [D&C 132:26] speaks of that obedience out of which eternal life grows, and still speaking both of celestial marriage and of making one's calling and election sure says: "Verily, verily, I say unto you, if a man marry a wife according to my word, and they are sealed by the Holy Spirit of promise, according to mine appointment"— that is, if they are both married and have their calling and election made sure . . . "they shall come forth in the first resurrection and enter into their exaltation."[14]

Second Comforter

Even after your calling and election has been made sure, there is even another step that you can take to grow in the light. Joseph Smith's words are helpful to see the transition from "calling and election" to this next most sacred event:

> After a person has faith in Christ, repents of his sins, and is baptized for the remission of his sins and receives the Holy Ghost, (by the laying on of hands), which is the first Comforter, then let him continue to humble himself before God, hungering and thirsting after righteousness, and living by every word of God, and *the Lord will soon say unto him, Son, thou shalt be exalted.* When the Lord has thoroughly proved him, and finds that the man is determined to serve Him at all hazards, *then the man will find his calling and his election made sure,* then it will be his *privilege to receive the other Comforter. . . .*
>
> *Now, what is this other Comforter? It is no more or less than the Lord Jesus Christ Himself;* and this is the sum and substance of the whole matter; that when any man obtains this *last Comforter,* he will have the *personage of Jesus Christ to attend him, or appear unto him from time to time,* and even He *will manifest the Father unto him . . .* and the visions of the heavens will be opened unto him; and *the Lord will teach him face to face.*[15]

In essence, this last Comforter, or second Comforter, is having our own First Vision experience. Speaking of the First Vision, one noted Latter-day Saint scholar observed: "Critics of the Church have made a lot of fuss about the fact that we have so few contemporary accounts of the First Vision. But that rather makes the point. Joseph was talking more about what we could do than what he had done. *We have a dozen revelations in the Doctrine and Covenants that invite us to see God. Joseph invited us to check him by having our own Sacred Grove experience.*"[16] A few examples from the Doctrine and Covenants that "invite us to see God" include (but are not limited to) the following:

> The appearing of the Father and the Son, in that verse [referring to John 14:23], is a *personal appearance;* and the idea that the Father and the Son dwell in a man's heart is an old sectarian notion, and is false. (D&C 130:3; emphasis added)

> Verily, thus saith the Lord: It shall come to pass that every soul who forsaketh his sins and cometh unto me, and calleth on my name, and obeyeth my voice, and keepeth my commandments, *shall see my face and know that I am.* (D&C 93:1; emphasis added)

And again, verily I say unto you that it is your privilege, and a promise I give unto you that have been ordained unto this ministry, that inasmuch as you strip yourselves from jealousies and fears, and humble yourselves before me, for ye are not sufficiently humble, the veil shall be rent and *you shall see me and know that I am*—not with the carnal neither natural mind, but with the spiritual.

For no man has seen God at any time in the flesh, except quickened by the Spirit of God. (D&C 67:10–11; emphasis added)

Therefore, sanctify yourselves that your minds become single to God, and *the days will come that you shall see him*; for he will unveil his face unto you, and it shall be in his own time, and in his own way, and according to his own will. (D&C 88:68; emphasis added)

Therefore, in the ordinances thereof, the power of godliness is manifest.

And without the ordinances thereof, and the authority of the priesthood, the power of godliness is not manifest unto men in the flesh;

For *without this no man can see the face of God*, even the Father, and live.

Now this Moses plainly taught to the children of Israel in the wilderness, and sought diligently to sanctify his people that they might behold the face of God;

But they hardened their hearts and could not endure his presence. (D&C 84:20–24; emphasis added)

Where and how this sacred event would occur is perhaps only known by those who receive it. However, perhaps this verse from the dedicatory prayer of the Kirtland Temple can give us a clue: "For thou knowest that we have done this work [building the temple] through great tribulation; and out of our poverty we have given of our substance to build a house [the temple] to thy name, *that the Son of Man might have a place to manifest himself to his people*" (D&C 109:5; emphasis added). Once again, we see how this last event, the second Comforter, is linked and woven into the tapestry of the House of the Lord, even the temple.

Joseph Smith once declared: "It is the first principle of the Gospel to know for a certainty the Character of God, and to know *that we may converse with him as one man converses with another*."[17] On another occasion, Joseph taught: "God hath not revealed anything to Joseph, but what He will make known unto the Twelve, and even the least Saint may know all things as fast as he is able to bear them."[18] This is to say, these various aspects of growing in the light of the temple are not limited to just high-ranking Church leaders. One of the beauties of Latter-day Saint theology and doctrine is its universality—these promises, however lofty, are intended for everyone, not just an elect few! Elder Boyd K. Packer perceptively observed:

> We lay no claim to being Apostles of the world—but of the Lord Jesus Christ. The test is not whether men will believe, but whether the Lord has called us—and of that there is no doubt! *We do not talk of those sacred interviews that qualify the servants of the Lord to bear a special witness of Him, for we have been commanded not to do so.* But we are free, indeed, we are obliged, to bear that special witness. But that witness, the testimony of this work, is not reserved to those few of us who lead the Church. *In proper order that witness comes to men and women and children all over the world.*[19]

It should be noted that although these promises can be received by anyone who is willing to receive them, they cannot and usually will not come except to those who genuinely live and grow in the Light of Christ throughout their life.

Conclusion

Many of these later steps in growing in the light do not come until after one has progressed and grown through many levels of light and spiritual illumination. "When you climb up a ladder," said Joseph Smith, "you must begin at the bottom, and ascend step by step, until you arrive at the top; and so it is with the principles of the gospel—you must begin with the first, and go on until you learn all the principles of exaltation. But it will be a great while after you have passed through the veil before you will have learned them. It is not all to be comprehended in this world; it will be a great work to learn our salvation and exaltation even beyond the grave."[20]

In this chapter, we have viewed the temple from the perspective of light and our growth in that light. In reality, this particular viewpoint is just another way of looking at the plan of salvation. In fact, it could be said that our growth in the light is really just an expression and realization of how we incorporate Christ's Atonement in our lives. Illustratively, President Henry B. Eyring once said that the "reception of the Holy Ghost is the cleansing agent as the atonement purifies you. . . . That is a fact you can act on with confidence. You can invite the Holy Ghost's companionship into your life. And you can know when he is there, and when he withdraws. And when he is your companion, you can have confidence that the Atonement is working in your life."[21] To the degree that we grow in the light, we also grow in the Atonement. As the light grows brighter and brighter, so does the applicable power of the Atonement grow in our lives. The degree that we apply the Atonement in our lives will determine our eternal reward.

Elder D. Todd Christofferson observed: "What endeavor is more magnificent than bringing the children of God to *ultimate salvation* through the grace of their Redeemer, the Lord Jesus Christ? . . . *Eternal life depends on the exercise of our moral agency, but it is possible only through the grace of Jesus Christ.*"[22] What a fascinating concept! Eternal life is not dependent on the amount of works we perform; it is dependent on how much of the Atonement we allow to access our souls. May we all strive to follow the admonition of Elder McConkie that he gave in the final discourse of his mortal ministry: "God grant that all of us may walk in the light as God our Father is in the light so that, according to the promises, the blood of Jesus Christ His Son will cleanse us from all sin."[23]

Notes

1. I am indebted to Larry Dahl, who introduced me to some of the framework that will be utilized in this chapter. His amiable and thoughtful tutelage while I was a religion teacher at BYU in 1998 is greatly appreciated.
2. C. S. Lewis, "Is Theology Poetry?" (presentation before the Oxford Socratic Club, Oxford University, England, 1944).
3. Gene R. Cook (to Religious Education Department, Brigham Young University, Park City, UT, September 1, 1989).
4. Francis M. Lyman, in Conference Report, April 1899, 37; emphasis added.
5. Joseph F. Smith, *Gospel Doctrine*, 5th ed. (1939), 67–68; emphasis added.
6. David A. Bednar, "Receive the Holy Ghost," *Ensign*, November 2010, 94; emphasis added.
7. David A. Bednar, "Clean Hands and a Pure Heart," *Ensign*, November 2007, 81; emphasis added.

8. Henry B. Eyring, "Dedicatory Prayer for the Indianapolis Indiana Temple," prayer offered August 23, 2015, lds.org; emphasis added.

9. Stephen E. Robinson, "Enduring to the End," *Ensign*, October 1993; emphasis added.

10. Bruce R. McConkie, *Doctrinal New Testament Commentary* (Salt Lake City: Bookcraft, 1973), 3:330–31.

11. See Topical Guide, "Calling and Election Sure" for a multitude of scriptural references.

12. "Come, Listen to a Prophet's Voice," *Hymns*, no. 21; emphasis added.

13. "I Believe in Christ," *Hymns*, no. 134; emphasis added.

14. Bruce R. McConkie, *Doctrinal New Testament Commentary* (Salt Lake City: Bookcraft, 1973), 3:343–44.

15. Joseph Smith, *Teachings of the Prophet Joseph Smith*, sel. Joseph Fielding Smith (1976), 150–51; emphasis added.

16. Joseph Fielding McConkie, *Regional Studies in Latter-day Saint Church History: Illinois* (Provo, UT: Brigham Young University, Department of Church History and Doctrine, 1995), 206–7; emphasis added.

17. Joseph Smith, *Teachings of the Prophet Joseph Smith*, sel. Joseph Fielding Smith (1976), 345; emphasis added.

18. Ibid, 149.

19. Boyd K. Packer, "A Tribute to the Rank and File of the Church," *Ensign*, May 1980, 62; emphasis added.

20. Joseph Smith, in *History of the Church*, 6:306–7.

21. Henry B. Eyring, "Come Unto Christ: The Atonement" (Brigham Young University fireside, October 29, 1989), speeches.byu.edu.

22. D. Todd Christofferson, "Why We Share the Gospel," *Ensign*, August 2014, 36–37; emphasis added.

23. Bruce R. McConkie, "The Purifying Power of Gethsemane," *Ensign*, May 1985, 11.

$\mathcal{N}ine$

"My Father's House": Patterns of Salvation in the Holy Temple

And if thou art faithful unto the end thou shalt have a crown of
immortality, and eternal life in the mansions which I have
prepared in the house of my Father. (D&C 81:6)

So far in this book, we have viewed the temple and much that pertains to it through the perspective of the Atonement of Jesus Christ. In this chapter, we seek to examine whose temple this really is and the true means by which salvation comes, mainly, our Father in Heaven.

Latter-day temples bear a familiar inscription: "Holiness to the Lord, The House of the Lord." Church members often refer to the temple simply as the "House of the Lord" or even "God's Holy House." Often we think the name "Lord" or "God" is referring to Jesus Christ, which it does in a sense. However, it is interesting that Christ Himself refers to the temple as "my father's house" in John 2:16. Truly the temple is the house of God, that is, God the Father.

The theology behind this description and reality is beautifully taught in the temple. This is to say, that all things begin and end with the Father. The overarching teaching from the temple is that this is the plan of God, the Father. He is in charge. All instructions relating to His plan derive from Him. He gives the commands, the directives, the instructions—the whole program follows His lead and reports back to Him as well. Christ is an important part of this plan, and thus He plays an important role in the theology of the temple. However, the doctrinal thrust of temple theology centers on God, the Father. In this chapter, we examine this unique and fundamental doctrine that is often misunderstood by Latter-day Saints. It is hoped that as this doctrine is better understood, there will be a greater appreciation for the temple and all doctrines, ordinances, and symbols that relate thereunto.

The Temple of Our Heavenly Father

Section 109 of the Doctrine and Covenants is a fascinating block of scripture relative to the temple. This section is the dedicatory prayer for the Kirtland Temple, the first temple of this last dispensation. Joseph Smith taught the Saints that this prayer was not a product of his own musings and ideas, but rather that it came through direct revelation from heaven. Within the first thirty-three verses, there are six examples that demonstrate that holy temple belongs to the "Holy Father" (see verses 4, 10, 14, 22, 24, and 29). At the very outset of the prayer, the plea is made thus: "And now we ask thee, *Holy Father*, in the name of Jesus Christ, the Son of thy bosom, *in whose name alone salvation can be administered* to the children of men, we ask thee, O Lord, to accept of this house, the workmanship of the hands of us, thy servants, *which thou didst command us to build*" (D&C 109:4; emphasis added). Clearly this is Heavenly Father's house and He commanded the Saints to build it. Jesus Christ bears a very important role in temple worship. In verse 4 we learn a powerful truth: salvation doesn't begin with Christ—it is facilitated through Christ, "*in whose name alone salvation can be administered.*"

Several years ago, I heard something very intriguing about this doctrine. I was in a meeting for Church religious educators where a guest speaker had been invited to give a presentation. He was from Church correlation, a department that, among other things, seeks to systematize and ensure the consistency in teaching and doctrinal purity within Church classes and their associated instruction manuals. Correlation is overseen by the First Presidency and Quorum of the Twelve. Our guest gave a nice overview of the history of the correlation department along with its beginnings, its intended purpose, and its current focus. Near the end of his presentation, he invited those of us gathered to engage in a question/answer session. At one point someone in our group asked: "Are there any current doctrinal concerns that the brethren have?" Our guest quickly responded with a resolute "yes!"

Over the next several minutes, he prefaced his remarks by explaining how much effort had been made by the Church and its members during the past several decades to place more of an emphasis on Christ. He cited examples of these efforts, including the change in the Church logo, the new subtitle of the Book of Mormon "Another Testament of Christ," and themes in conference talks and Church magazines that emphasize Christ and His redeeming powers. He then went on to say that members also had caught the spirit of this emphasis: increased discussion on Christ in lessons, portrayals of Christ and His Atonement through books, music, and stage productions, etc.

Then came his answer to the original question: he explained that although the brethren are pleased with this renewed emphasis on the Savior, their fear, in his view, is that we as a Church are forgetting to make appropriate emphasis on such issues as the power, the might, the love, and the redeeming abilities of the Father, our Heavenly Father.

At first I was a bit baffled, not quite sure what he meant. I always had taught (and had heard from others) about Christ having the power to save; He has the power to redeem; He has the power to resurrect people, etc. Yet now there was more that I realized I had not fully known or considered. My discovery that day and my subsequent study of the scriptures of the Restoration yielded insights that helped me gain a greater appreciation for one of the key foundational doctrines of the Restoration related to the Godhead. I was filled with excitement and began to see immediate connections to other scriptures and doctrines.

These newfound and clarifying insights prompted me to look at certain scripture blocks in ways that I had never considered. I felt, perhaps in a smaller way, how Joseph Smith once felt as he described his experience shortly after being baptized by and with Oliver Cowdery: "Our minds being now enlightened, we began to have the scriptures laid open to our understandings, and the true meaning and intention of their . . . passages revealed unto us in a manner which we never could attain to previously, nor ever before had thought of" (Joseph Smith—History 1:74).

The Fatherhood of Jesus Christ

It should be clarified prior to developing this chapter further that there are many instances where the term *Father* is employed in scriptures of the Restoration in referring to the doctrine of the fatherhood of Jesus Christ, as opposed to simply denoting *Heavenly Father*. Although the thrust of this article is to examine those references relating directly with Heavenly Father and His salvific works and acts, a few examples of scriptures referring the Fatherhood of Christ will be mentioned so as to delineate this specific usage from the stated theme.

Jesus Christ is referred to as the Father for several reasons.[1] First, Jesus is the Father in the sense that He is *Father of Creation*. King Benjamin's words are a helpful illustration of this point: "And he shall be called Jesus Christ, the Son of God, *the Father of heaven and earth*, the Creator of all things from the beginning; and his mother shall be called Mary" (Mosiah 3:8; emphasis added). Christ's title as Father of Creation is similar to the way one would refer to George Washington as the father of our nation—it is symbolic in meaning.

Second, Jesus Christ is the Father of our spiritual rebirth. To be clear, Jesus is not the Father of our spirits. That title is reserved for and exclusively applied to our Heavenly Father as the literal parent who begets our individual spirits. However, it is appropriate to refer to Christ as *Father* in the sense that we become His offspring, symbolically speaking, when we enter into a covenant relationship through the waters of baptism and the reception of the Holy Ghost.

King Benjamin's words, once again, are helpful in illustrating this second point: "And now, *because of the covenant* which ye have made ye shall be called *the children of Christ, his sons, and his daughters*; for behold, this day *he hath spiritually begotten you*; for ye say that your hearts are changed through faith on his name; therefore, *ye are born of him and have become his sons and his daughters*" (Mosiah 5:7; emphasis added).

Third, Jesus is the Father by a principle known as Divine Investiture of Authority. This is to say that in "all His dealings with the human family Jesus the Son has represented and yet represents Elohim His Father in power and authority. . . . The Father placed His name upon the Son; and Jesus Christ spoke and ministered in and through the Father's name; and so far as power, authority and Godship are concerned His words and acts were and are those of the Father."[2] Elder Larry E. Dahl further describes this type of Fatherhood possessed by the Son by saying: "It may be in many of the scriptures where it appears the Father is speaking that Jesus Christ is really the voice, speaking in the name of the Father in the first person as if he were the Father."[3] There may even be other scriptural reasons to refer to Christ as Father, however the preceding examples should be sufficient to make the desired point.[4]

By the Power of the Father

Jesus Christ rightly bears the titles of Savior and Redeemer. Although true that He performs (and has and will yet perform) many salvific works (which he often does in and through the appropriately applied title of Father as stated previously), nevertheless, His redeeming and saving powers are not without precedent or source. A close reading of the Gospel of John is helpful in understanding this doctrine. In John 5, the Savior clearly teaches the relationship that exists between him and the Father. Jesus said: "The Son can do nothing of himself. . . . I can of mine own self do nothing" (John 5:19, 30). Although unintentionally, some might erroneously consider the Son as the exclusive source of salvation while viewing Heavenly Father as a detached bystander who, with anxiety, relies solely on the Son to perform a litany of redemptive acts. In speaking of a correct understanding of the plan of salvation, especially in the premortal existence, Elder Bruce R. McConkie taught this doctrine:

> One of the saddest examples of a misconceived and twisted knowledge of an otherwise glorious concept is the all-too-common heresy that there were two plans of salvation; that the Father (presumptively at a loss to know what to do) asked others for proposals; that Christ offered a plan involving agency and Lucifer proposed a plan denying agency; that the Father chose between them; and that Lucifer, his plan being rejected, rebelled, and then there was war in heaven.
>
> Even a cursory knowledge of the overall scheme of things reassures spiritually discerning persons that all things center in the Father; that *the plan of salvation which he designed was to save his children, Christ included; and that neither Christ nor Lucifer could of themselves save anyone.* . . .
>
> There is, of course, a sense in which we may refer to Lucifer's proposed modifications of the Father's plan as Lucifer's plan, and Christ made the Father's plan his own by adoption. But what is basically important in this respect is to know that *the power to save is vested in the Father,* and that he originated, ordained, created, and established his own plan; that he announced it to his children; and that he then asked for a volunteer to be the Redeemer, the Deliverer, *the Messiah, who would put the eternal plan of the Eternal Father into eternal operation.*[5]

Thus it is that the power to save (in any fashion) is vested in, originates from, and derives itself in the first instance from *the* Father, our Father in Heaven. Ironically then, even Christ, who activates that operational effects of the Atonement through His sacrifice, is dependent upon the power that issues from Heavenly Father. What then are all of the fashions that the Father, our Heavenly Father, saves his children? The following is a brief look at seven examples taught clearly from scriptures of the Restoration.

(1) Power to Resurrect—Salvation from Physical Death

It is often the case in Church classes when the Resurrection is taught that instructors will teach or claim that Christ resurrected Himself, that He had power in and of Himself to die and to be resurrected. Often these verses are cited as scriptural support: "Therefore doth my Father love me, because I lay down my life, that I might take it again. No man taketh it from me, but I lay it down of myself. *I have power to lay it down, and I have power to take it again.* This commandment have I received of my Father" (John 10:17–18; emphasis added). From this some might conclude that Christ had the inherent power within Himself to resurrect Himself. True it is that He was the first of all of Heavenly Father's children to be resurrected, and that He became "the firstfruits of them that slept" and that "by man came death [and] by man came also the resurrection of the dead. For as in Adam all die, even so in Christ shall all be made alive" (1 Corinthians 15:20–22).

However, a further reading of these verses in 1 Corinthians informs us that Heavenly Father "raised up Christ" in the first instance (1 Corinthians 15:15). Scriptures of the Restoration confirm and further amplify this teaching. In some of his final instructive words to his son Moroni, the prophet Mormon counseled: "Know ye that ye must come to the knowledge of your fathers, and repent of all your sins and iniquities, and believe in Jesus Christ, that he is the Son of God, and that he was slain by the Jews, and *by the power of the Father he hath risen again,* whereby he hath gained the victory over the grave; and also in him is the sting of death swallowed up" (Mormon 7:5; emphasis added).

Thus it is that Christ didn't in reality resurrect Himself by his own power but rather through the power of the Father. Not only does the power to resurrect come through the Father, but likewise through the same power the Son is thus able to serve as our advocate or intermediary with the Father: "Yea, even so he [Christ] shall be led, crucified, and slain, the flesh becoming subject even unto death, the will of the Son being swallowed up in the will of the Father. And *thus God [the Father] breaketh the bands of death,* having gained the victory over death; *giving the*

Son power to make intercession for the children of men" (Mosiah 15:7–8; emphasis added).

In speaking of those that were gathered together in the spirit world to receive instruction and to be commissioned to preach to the spirits in prison, President Joseph F. Smith described in his vision that all these righteous spirits "had departed the mortal life, firm in the hope of *a glorious resurrection, through the grace of God the Father* and his Only Begotten Son, Jesus Christ" (D&C 138:14; emphasis added).

(2) Power to Remit Sins

It is evident that the power of the resurrection comes from the Father, but what about the power to remit sins? Interestingly, the power for the redemption from sin likewise comes through the Father:

> And remember also the words which Amulek spake unto Zeezrom, in the city of Ammonihah; for he said unto him that the Lord surely should come to redeem his people, but that he should not come to redeem them in their sins, but to redeem them from their sins.
>
> And *he [Christ] hath power given unto him from the Father to redeem* them from their sins because of repentance; therefore he hath sent his angels to declare the tidings of the conditions of repentance, which bringeth unto the power of the Redeemer, unto the salvation of their souls. (Helaman 5:10–11; emphasis added)

Not only does the power to remit sins reside with the Father but so does the power to forgive: "For, if ye forgive men their trespasses *your heavenly Father will also forgive you*; But if ye forgive not men their trespasses neither will your Father forgive your trespasses" (3 Nephi 13:14–15; emphasis added). Likewise, it is through the Father that a person is not only forgiven but ultimately sanctified from sinfulness. The Resurrected Christ prayed thus: "Father, I thank thee *that thou hast purified those whom I have chosen*, because of their faith, and I pray for them, and also for them who shall believe on their words, that they may be purified in me, through faith on their words, even as they are purified in me" (3 Nephi 19:28; emphasis added).

(3) Power to Exalt

Another related principle is also taught in the scriptures relative to the Father's power; that is, not only does the Father have the power to resurrect and to redeem from sin, but also to ultimately save and exalt mankind in the highest degree of the Celestial world. This truth is illustrated beautifully in the New Testament. In Matthew 20:20–23, an interesting dialogue occurs between Christ and a certain woman:

> Then came to him the mother of Zebedee's children with her sons, worshipping him, and desiring a certain thing of him.
>
> And he said unto her, What wilt thou? She saith unto him, Grant that these my two sons may sit, the one on thy right hand, and the other on the left, in thy kingdom.
>
> But Jesus answered and said, Ye know not what ye ask. Are ye able to drink of the cup that I shall drink of, and to be baptized with the baptism that I am baptized with? They say unto him, We are able.
>
> And he saith unto them, Ye shall drink indeed of my cup, and be baptized with the baptism that I am baptized with: *but to sit on my right hand, and on my left, is not mine to give, but it shall be given to them for whom it is prepared of my Father.* (emphasis added)

The scriptures of the Restoration likewise attest that it is indeed the Father that exalts mankind and grants to them an inheritance of eternal life.

> And thus we saw the glory of the celestial, which excels in all things— where *God, even the Father,* reigns upon his throne forever and ever;
>
> Before whose throne [God the Father's throne] all things bow in humble reverence, and give him [God, the Father] glory forever and ever.
>
> They who dwell in his [God, the Father's] presence are the church of the Firstborn; and they see as they are seen, and know as they are known, *having received of his [the father's] fulness and of his grace;*
>
> And *he [the Father] makes them* equal in power, and in might, and in dominion. (D&C 76:92–95; emphasis added; see also D&C 66:12, 84:38, and 109:71)

Likewise the Book of Mormon testifies of this truth: "And for this cause *ye shall have fulness of joy*; and ye shall sit down in the *kingdom of my Father*; yea, your joy shall be full, *even as the Father hath given me fulness of joy*; and ye shall be even as I am, and I am even as the Father; and the Father and I are one" (3 Nephi 28:10; emphasis added). Yes, the Father has power to save, to forgive, to redeem, etc.—but He also has the power and ability to give ultimate salvation in His kingdom. "And who overcome by faith, and are sealed by the Holy Spirit of promise, *which the Father sheds forth* upon all those who are just and true. They are they who are the church of the Firstborn. They are they *into whose hands the Father has given all* things—They are they who are priests and kings, who have *received of his fulness, and of his glory*" (D&C 76:53–56; emphasis added).

(4) Power to Bestow the Holy Ghost

Even the gift of the Holy Ghost comes ultimately through the agency and might of the Father: "And also, the voice of the Son came unto me, saying: He that is baptized in my name, *to him will the Father give the Holy Ghost*, like unto me; wherefore, follow me, and do the things which ye have seen me do" (2 Nephi 31:12; emphasis added). The Savior likewise taught His chosen disciples in the Americas that "*the Father giveth the Holy Ghost* unto the children of men" (3 Nephi 28:11; emphasis added). "Father, I pray thee that *thou wilt give the Holy Ghost* unto all them that shall believe in me. *Father, thou hast given them the Holy Ghost* because they believe in me; and thou seest that they believe in me because thou hearest them, and they pray unto me; and they pray unto me because I am with them" (3 Nephi 19:21–22; emphasis added). It is interesting to note that the power of the Holy Ghost, which can come upon one before baptism and serves the purpose of verifying truth, also comes through the power of the Father: "And behold, this is the thing which I will give unto you for a sign—for verily I say unto you that when these things which I declare unto you, and which I shall declare unto you hereafter of myself, and *by the power of the Holy Ghost which shall be given unto you of the Father*, shall be made known *unto the Gentiles*" (3 Nephi 21:2; emphasis added).

(5) Power to Bring Mankind to Judgment

Ultimately, all men and women will not only be resurrected by the power of the Father as previously stated, but also through His power they will be brought back into His presence, whether good or bad for the final judgment:

> Behold I have given unto you my gospel, and this is the gospel which I have given unto you—that *I came into the world to do the will of my Father*, because my Father sent me.
>
> And my Father sent me that I might be lifted up upon the cross; and after that I had been lifted up upon the cross, that I might draw all men unto me, that as I have been lifted up by men even *so should men be lifted up by the Father, to stand before me, to be judged of their works*, whether they be good or whether they be evil—

And for this cause have I been lifted up; therefore, *according to the power of the Father I will draw all men unto me, that they may be judged* according to their works. (3 Nephi 27:13–15; emphasis added)

To the unrepented Nephites who suffered great destruction almost four hundred years after Christ's appearance at the temple in Bountiful, Mormon taught and lamented: "The Father, yea, the *Eternal Father of heaven*, knoweth your state; and he *doeth with you according to his justice and mercy*" (Mormon 6:22; emphasis added).

In the vision where he saw the three degrees of glory, Joseph Smith taught that "these are they whose names are written in heaven, where *God and Christ are the judge of all*" (D&C 76:68; emphasis added).

(6) Power to Assist us to Endure to the End

It is likewise through the power, grace, and assistance of the Father that we are enabled to endure to the end. In one of his last, solitary epistles to his son Moroni, the prophet Mormon counseled: "I am mindful of you always in my prayers, continually praying unto *God the Father* in the name of *his Holy Child*, Jesus, that he [the Father], through *his infinite goodness and grace* [that of the Father], will keep you through the endurance of faith on his name to the end" (Moroni 8:3; emphasis added; see also 3 Nephi 27:6–17).

(7) Power to Restore the Gospel

It could be argued that even the determination and facilitation of such epochal events as the Restoration of the gospel and the gathering are made in and through the knowledge, power, and authority of the Father: "When they therefore were come together, they asked of him, saying, Lord, wilt thou at this time restore again the kingdom to Israel? And he said unto them, It is not for you to know the times or the seasons, *which the Father hath put in his own power*" (Acts 1:6–7; emphasis added). In speaking to the Nephites, the Savior reminds them of the covenants the Father has made regarding the restoration of Israel in the last days:

And it shall come to pass that the time cometh, when the fulness of my gospel shall be preached unto them;

And they shall believe in me, that I am Jesus Christ, the Son of God, and shall pray unto the Father in my name.

Then shall their watchmen lift up their voice, and with the voice together shall they sing; for they shall see eye to eye.

Then will the Father gather them together again, and give unto them Jerusalem for the land of their inheritance.

Then shall they break forth into joy—Sing together, ye waste places of Jerusalem; *for the Father hath comforted his people, he hath redeemed Jerusalem.*

The Father hath made bare his holy arm in the eyes of all the nations; and all the ends of the earth shall see *the salvation of the Father*; and the Father and I are one. (3 Nephi 20:30–35; emphasis added)

Perhaps all of this is one of the reasons the Savior teaches this difficult and perplexing concept in Matthew 19:16–17: "And, behold, one came and said unto him, Good Master, what good thing shall I do, that I may have eternal life? And he said unto him, Why callest thou me good? [there is] none good but one, [that is], God: but if thou wilt enter into life, keep the commandments." Obviously Jesus was a "good" person by anyone's standards. In fact, we might be prone to say that this is an extreme example (or portrayal) of self-modesty on the part of the Master. However, from the perspective that we have previously articulated, we can see that His words are true—that is to say, there is no one apart from God the Father who can save! No one is "good" enough in and of himself to "save himself," not even Christ, who interestingly, could not save Himself apart from the power granted to Him from His Father. "The plan of salvation originated with the Father," said Elder Bruce R. McConkie, "he is the Author and Finisher of our faith in the final sense." Elder McConkie further noted that "it is the Father's gospel, it became the gospel of the Son by adoption, and we call it after Christ's name because his atoning sacrifice put all of its terms and conditions into operation."[6]

Truly it is through the grace, mercy, and power of God the Father (which is then delegated, extended, and facilitated through the Son) that we are all convinced, empowered, cleansed, forgiven, changed, resurrected, saved, and exalted. These truths are evidenced in words from a modern apostle: "A Christian believes *that through the grace of God the Father* and His Son, Jesus Christ, *we can repent, forgive others, keep the commandments, and inherit eternal life.*"[7]

Grace for Grace

In this chapter, we have discussed the concept of grace as it applies to Heavenly Father. Often we teach or think that grace is completely a function of Christ extending His grace and mercy to us. It is true that certain blessings come "through the grace and mercy" of Christ (see D&C 20:30–31), but this is not to say that Christ has always been a possessor of all goodness, grace, and mercy. "But we see Jesus, who was made a little lower than the angels for the suffering of death, crowned with glory and honour; *that he by the grace of God* should taste death for every man" (Hebrews 2:9; emphasis added). Once again, it is by the grace and mercy of God the Father from whence all blessings and benefits to mankind are bestowed.

In section 93 of the Doctrine and Covenants, we learn that Christ and the Father "are one" (verse 3) because the "Father . . . gave [Christ] of his [the Father's] fullness" (verse 4). Christ, then, being our advocate and mediator with the Father, "was the Word, even the messenger of salvation" (verse 8), which would be a fitting title: He is not the source of salvation, but the messenger thereof. Section 93 continues: "And I, John, saw that *he received not of the fulness at the first, but received grace for grace*; And he received not of the fulness at first, but continued from grace to grace, until he received a fulness; And thus he was called the Son of God, because he received not of the fulness at the first" (verses 12–14; emphasis added).

Apparently it was not until Christ was baptized that He received a fulness of the Father: "And I, John, bear record, and lo, the heavens were opened, and the Holy Ghost descended upon him in the form of a dove, and sat upon him, and there came a voice out of heaven saying: This is my beloved Son. And I, John, bear record that *he received a fulness of the glory of the Father*; and *he received all power, both in heaven and on earth, and the glory of the Father was with him*, for he dwelt in him" (D&C 93:15–17; emphasis added).

We further learned that if we are faithful, we too can one day have the same that the Son has received: "I give unto you these sayings that you may understand and know how to worship, and know what you worship, that you may come unto the Father in my name, and *in due time receive of his fulness. For if you keep my commandments you shall receive of his fulness, and be glorified in me as I am in the Father; therefore, I say unto you, you shall receive grace for grace*" (D&C 93:19–20; emphasis added). The power to save then, as Elder McConkie has stated, is not vested in the Son, but in the Father, and is bestowed upon the Son. If we are true and faithful, that same power to save will be bestowed upon us as we begin the cycle of "eternal increase." It could well be that one day, as exalted, glorified beings, we will have "all power" to save our spirit children, just as it is ultimately our Heavenly Father who has the power to redeem, save, resurrected, perfect, and exalt His children (D&C 131:1–4; see also D&C 132:19–22, 84:33–39, and 78:15–16).

It is interesting to note that Christ thus grows "grace for grace"—this is to say that He grows by the very power that issues from His atoning sacrifice, which power in reality emanates from the Father.

All of this raises an interesting question: Was Jesus Christ perfect while in His mortal state? If one examines Matthew 5:48 and 3 Nephi 12:48 the answer is apparently "no." This is because Jesus was not yet "complete, finished, fully developed" (see Matthew 5:48, footnote *b*) until He was resurrected. No, Jesus was not perfect, yet He was "sinless" as the scriptures attest (see 1 John 3:5; 1 Peter 2:22; Hebrews 4:15; D&C 45:4). President Lorenzo Snow once stated:

> When Jesus lay in the manger, a helpless infant, He knew not that He was the Son of God, and that formerly He created the earth. When the edict of Herod was issued, He knew nothing of it; He had not power to save Himself; and His father and mother had to take Him and fly into Egypt to preserve Him from the effects of that edict. Well, He grew up to manhood, and during His progress it was revealed unto Him who He was, and for what purpose He was in the world. *The glory and power He possessed before He came into the world was made known unto Him.*[8]

One commentator has observed:

> The Savior increased in grace as he lived the commandments of God and blessed the lives of others. His growth was accelerated above that of his fellowmen because of the reciprocal nature of receiving strength of the Spirit when extending grace. That is, he called upon his Father for power and strength to bless others in their need. In answer to his prayers, he was empowered and grew beyond his previous abilities, thus, receiving grace *for* grace. Christ was foremost in reaching out in compassion to others. Therefore, he received greater grace from God in his efforts than any other person.[9]

3 Nephi 21: A Case Study on the Power of the Father

The entirety of 3 Nephi 21 is an excellent illustration of the fact that all things center in the power of the Father. As we have established previously, we learn truly that "the power of the Holy Ghost [is] given unto [us] of the Father" (3 Nephi 21:2). It is by the "wisdom in the Father" that various groups or peoples are "established in this land [the Americas], and [are] set up as a free people by the power of the Father" (3 Nephi 21:4). It thus "behooveth the Father that it should come forth from the Gentiles, that he may show forth his power unto the Gentiles, for this cause that the Gentiles, if they will not harden their hearts, that they may repent and come unto me and be baptized in my name and know of the true points of my doctrine, that they may be numbered among my people" (3 Nephi 21:6).

Furthermore we learn that "the work of the Father hath already commenced unto the fulfilling of the covenant which he hath made unto the people who are of the house of Israel" (3 Nephi 21:7). Additionally, "the Father shall cause him [Jesus Christ] to bring forth [the Father's word] unto the Gentiles, and shall give unto him [Christ] power that he shall bring them forth unto the Gentiles" (3 Nephi 21:11). A warning is given by the Father "that all lyings, and deceivings, and envyings, and strifes, and priestcrafts, and whoredoms, shall be done away [or else] it shall come to pass, saith the Father, that at that day whosoever will not repent and come unto my Beloved Son, them will I cut off from among my people, O house of Israel" (3 Nephi 21:19–20). But if the people of this land "repent and hearken unto my words, and harden not their hearts, I [the Father] will establish my church among them" (3 Nephi 21:22).

> And then shall the work of the Father commence at that day, even when this gospel shall be preached among the remnant of this people. Verily I say unto you, at that day shall the work of the Father commence among all the dispersed of my people, yea, even the tribes which have been lost, which the Father hath led away out of Jerusalem.
>
> Yea, the work shall commence among all the dispersed of my people, with the Father to prepare the way whereby they may come unto me, that they may call on the Father in my name.
>
> Yea, and then shall the work commence, with the Father among all nations in preparing the way whereby his people may be gathered home to the land of their inheritance. And they shall go out from all

nations; and they shall not go out in haste, nor go by flight, for I will go before them, saith the Father, and I will be their rearward. (3 Nephi 21:26–28)

Conclusion

Ultimately, salvation is centered in the Father. In this chapter we have examined the fact that salvation, in any form, comes in and through, by and from, our Father in Heaven. It is true that Jesus has received a fulness of this power from the Father, and that through His infinite and atoning sacrifice He has made the powers of redemption operative and efficacious for "all men if they will hearken unto his voice; for behold, he suffereth the pains of all men, yea, the pains of every living creature, both men, women, and children, who belong to the family of Adam" (2 Nephi 9:21). Christ not only has an infinite and eternal love for Father's children here on earth, but He loves, adores, follows, and worships the Father.

In John chapters 14 through 17, often known as the Intercessory Prayer, the Savior consistently and repeatedly refers to His Father. One who closely reads this block of scripture comes to understand that Christ not only *referenced* His Father, but He *reverenced* Him as well. One readily sees that Jesus's regard for the Father was *deferential* as well as *preferential*.

We often talk about the virtue of being disciples of Christ. This is important and a worthy goal to become such. But we must also understand that Christ was a disciple too—mainly, a disciple of His Father. A *disciple*, by simple definition, is a follower. He is a person who studies and exemplifies the teachings and doctrines of another. Thus Jesus Christ was a follower and a learner of the teachings and doctrines of His Father, our Father in Heaven. The Savior not only had studied and practiced the virtues of Father but He also came to earth to act Him out in such a way that we might understand and comprehend who the Father really is through the life and example of the Son. It could be said that Christ's mission to earth wasn't just to perform the Atonement for sin. If that weren't enough, Christ also came to manifest the Father, through His example, to mankind.

Elder Jeffrey R. Holland once taught:

Of the many magnificent purposes served in the life and ministry of the Lord Jesus Christ, one great aspect of that mission often goes uncelebrated. His followers did not understand it fully at the time, and many in modern Christianity do not grasp it now, but the Savior

Himself spoke of it repeatedly and emphatically. It is the grand truth that in all that Jesus came to say and do, including and especially in His atoning suffering and sacrifice, He was showing us who and what God our Eternal Father is like, how completely devoted He is to His children in every age and nation. In word and in deed Jesus was trying to reveal and make personal to us the true nature of His Father, our Father in Heaven.[10]

In simple terms, to know Christ is to know the Father (see John 8:19, 14:17, and 1 John 2:23). To partake of Christ's Redemption is, in reality, to partake of the salvation of the Father. To be loved so tenderly by Christ is to be loved with an infinite, eternal, and unchanging love by the Father. Perhaps it will come to pass in the next life that those who have felt somewhat alienated from the Father will realize that they have known Him all along, at least to the degree to which they have known and followed the Son. Perhaps those who have held the view that God is a distant, untouchable, and unknowable being will come to see that they understand and can relate to Him in very poignant, powerful, and personal ways. Ezra Taft Benson remarked that "nothing is going to startle us more when we pass through the veil to the other side than to realize how well we know our Father and how familiar his face is to us."[11] May we all, one day, "dwell in the presence of God in his kingdom, to sing ceaseless praises with the choirs above, unto the Father, and unto the Son, and unto the Holy Ghost, which are one God, in a state of happiness which hath no end" (Mormon 7:7).

Notes

1. The first three examples that will be shown herein are often illustrated through the document by the First Presidency and Council of the Twelve Apostles, "The Father and the Son: A Doctrinal Exposition by the First Presidency and the Twelve," *Improvement Era*, August 1916, 934–42. See also as recorded in James R. Clark, *Messages of the First Presidency*, 6 vols. (Salt Lake City: Bookcraft, 1971), 5:25–34.

2. "The Father and the Son: A Doctrinal Exposition by the First Presidency and the Twelve," *Improvement Era*, August 1916, 939–40.

3. Larry E. Dahl, "'The Morning Breaks, the Shadows Flee,'" *Ensign*, April 1997, 16.

4. Perhaps two more reasons could be added to the previous three for a total of five instances in the scriptures where Christ is referred to or treated as the Father. See Paul Y. Hoskisson, "The Fatherhood of Christ and the Atonement," in *Religious Educator* 1, no. 1 (2000): 71–80.

5. Bruce R. McConkie, *The Mortal Messiah: From Bethlehem to Calvary*, 4 vols. (Salt Lake City: Deseret Book Co., 1979–1981), 1:47.

6. Bruce R. McConkie, "Our Relationship with the Lord" (Brigham Young University devotional, March 2, 1982), 3, speeches.byu.edu.

7. Robert D. Hales, "Being a More Christian Christian," *Ensign*, November 2012, 90; emphasis added.

8. Lorenzo Snow, in Conference Report, April 1901, 3; emphasis added.

9. Joseph Fielding McConkie and Craig J. Ostler, *Revelations of the Restoration* (Salt Lake City: Deseret Book, 2000), 672–73.

10. Jeffrey R. Holland, "The Grandeur of God," *Ensign*, November 2003, 70.

11. Ezra Taft Benson, "Jesus Christ—Gifts and Expectations," in *Speeches of the Year, 1974* (Provo, UT: Brigham Young University Press, 1975), 313.

Ten

Temple Worthiness, Temple Blessings

And inasmuch as my people build a house unto me in the name of the Lord, and do not suffer any unclean thing to come into it, that it be not defiled, my glory shall rest upon it; Yea, and my presence shall be there, for I will come into it, and all the pure in heart that shall come into it shall see God. But if it be defiled I will not come into it, and my glory shall not be there; for I will not come into unholy temples.
(D&C 97:15–17)

While serving as a bishop several years ago, I had an intriguing conversation with a young man in our congregation. He had scheduled an appointment to speak with me. He was a return missionary and had been home for over a year. He was active in the Church and well-liked by the rest of his peer group. At first I could tell he was perplexed, his soul was heavy. He had come to confess some sins. I listened with patience and concern as he revealed some minor moral transgressions with which he had been struggling. After pouring out his heart and soul, he then revealed that he had not had any struggles for the past three months as he had tried on his own to abandon some bad habits. I praised him for his accomplishment and encouraged him to go forward with faith and hope. Then something interesting happened. Almost as an afterthought he added:

"Oh, and Bishop, I want you to know that I have not been taking the sacrament nor I have I gone to the temple."

His tone of rectitude was what caught my attention. In essence he was trying to suggest that, although he had sinned, he still had the decency and integrity to not participate in spiritual activities that he knew with certainty he was somehow unworthy. With a tone of love, yet still with curiosity and puzzlement, I asked:

"Oh, I see. Who told you not to take the sacrament or to not go to the temple?" He was instantly shocked.

"Well I knew that while sinning I shouldn't do those things. I figured after I stopped that it would be a long while before I was worthy again." Then with uncertainty he continued, "Was I not supposed to make that decision?" I told him he was not ever to make that decision on his own. I asked him if he knew whose responsibility it was to decide on his worthiness. With the same uncertainty he replied, "Is it you?" I acknowledged in the affirmative. He apologized and said he wouldn't do that again, but I could tell he was still confused for doing something that he thought demonstrated honesty. We talked for a bit until he understood the stewardship I had as his bishop in the role as a "judge in Israel." Then came the kicker. He looked at me with the most genuine, sincere, and contrite expression and asked, "How much longer should I not take the sacrament?" Now I was stunned, and I have to admit, almost on the verge of laughing.

With a slightly elevated, direct tone I asked, "Now let me see, you are not committing this sin anymore and have not done so for several months?" He agreed. I then asked what the sacrament symbolized. He replied that it was flesh and blood of the Savior. I nodded in agreement but then asked, "But what does it symbolize by taking those emblems inside of you?" He thought for a moment.

"I suppose it could mean that I want His Atonement in my life." He spoke with the spirit and humility. My next response was filled love, concern, and a bit of sarcasm:

"Do you?" I asked.

"Yes . . . yes, Bishop, I really do!"

"Then I want you to start taking the sacrament today at church, and I want you to go to the temple as soon as possible. Hopefully this week." My voice now beamed with confidence, support, and love for him. Tears welled up in his eyes. He then placed his head down into his cupped hands. After a moment he lifted his head back up, and looking me in the eyes, he said:

"But, Bishop, I'm not perfect!"

"Neither am I," I responded, "welcome to the club!"

Defining Worthiness

As we conclude this book on temple symbolism as it relates to Christ's Atonement, it might be helpful to discuss for a moment what worthiness really means. I have no right to speak for the entire Church on this matter, but it does seem to me to be helpful to mention a few principles that scriptures and our Church leaders have taught about these matters. In the Doctrine and Covenants, the Lord instructs the Saints:

> And inasmuch as my people build a house unto me in the name of the Lord, and *do not suffer any unclean thing to come into it, that it be not defiled*, my glory shall rest upon it; Yea, and my presence shall be there, for I will come into it, and all the pure in heart that shall come into it shall see God. *But if it be defiled I will not come into it, and my glory shall not be there; for I will not come into unholy temples.* (D&C 97:15–17; emphasis added)

To be certain, worthiness is a serious thing, and we should be worthy not only to enter the temple but also to take the sacrament. When the Savior visited the Nephites, He instituted, among other things, the blessing and administration of the sacrament. After preparing and administering the same, he then made this interesting declaration:

> And now behold, this is the commandment which I give unto you, that *ye shall not suffer any one knowingly to partake of my flesh and blood unworthily*, when ye shall minister it;
>
> For whoso eateth and drinketh my flesh and blood unworthily eateth and drinketh damnation to his soul; *therefore if ye know that a man is unworthy to eat and drink of my flesh and blood ye shall forbid him.* (3 Nephi 18:28–29; emphasis added)

I often will bait my students in Church Educational System (CES) classes with this scripture by asking them what they would do if they really knew that a person next to them was unworthy to take the sacrament but started to take it anyway. Would you slap their hand? Or simply shout out as they lift the bread to their mouth: "Bishop! Hurry, over here! Quick, we need a disciplinary council!" All humor aside, I challenge my students with this query. Most don't know what to say and even feel uncomfortable with the thought. Some say they probably would just talk with their friend in private. Others have responded that they wouldn't have the courage to fulfill the Savior's request. Then, we discuss the principle. I invite them to go to the beginning of 3 Nephi 18 so we can read the scripture in context:

> And it came to pass that Jesus commanded *his disciples* that they should bring forth some bread and wine unto him.
>
> And while they were gone for bread and wine, he commanded *the multitude* that they should sit themselves down upon the earth.
>
> And when *the disciples* had come with bread and wine, he took of the bread and brake and blessed it; and he gave unto *the disciples* and commanded that they should eat.
>
> And when they had eaten and were filled, he commanded that they should give *unto the multitude*.
>
> And *when the multitude* had eaten and were filled, *he said unto the disciples*: . . .
>
> And it came to pass that when he said these words, *he commanded his disciples* that they should take of the wine of the cup and drink of it, and that they should *also give unto the multitude* that they might drink of it.
>
> And it came to pass that they did so, and did drink of it and were filled; and *they gave unto the multitude*, and they did drink, and they were filled.
>
> And *when the disciples* had done this, Jesus said unto them: Blessed are ye for this thing which ye have done, for this is fulfilling my commandments, and this doth witness unto the Father that ye are willing to do that which I have commanded you. (3 Nephi 18:1–5, 8–10; emphasis added)

The Savior here is teaching and administering intermittently and alternately between two groups: the multitude, which is the general, large group gathered there with Him; and, the disciples, or in other words, his ecclesiastical leaders. By the time we arrive at verse 26 it reads as follows: "And now it came to pass that when Jesus had spoken these words, *he turned his eyes again upon the disciples whom he had chosen, and said unto them*" (3 Nephi 18:26, emphasis added). He then gives the command we referenced earlier with regards to prohibiting the sacrament to those who are not worthy. In other words, this command is only for Church officers in the performance of their rightful stewardships.

Elder Dallin H. Oaks confirms this teaching and principle thus:

We should not presume to exercise and act upon judgments that are outside our personal responsibilities. Some time ago I attended and adult Sunday school class in a small town in Utah. The subject was the sacrament and the class was being taught by the bishop. During class discussion a member asked, "What if you see an unworthy person partaking of the sacrament? What do you do?" The bishop answered, "You do nothing. I may need to do something." That wise answer illustrates my point about stewardship in judging.[1]

Not only should we not judge others, we should likewise take care never to judge our own worthiness. Elder Marvin J. Ashton once gave this illustration:

> Over the past number of weeks I have had some conversations that have made me ponder the meaning of the word *worthy*. As I recently talked to a young twenty-year-old man, I discussed his attitude about going on a mission. He said, "I wanted to go, but I am not worthy."
>
> "Who made that judgment?" I asked.
>
> "I did," was his answer.
>
> On another occasion I asked a young lady who was contemplating marriage if she was going to the temple. She said, "I would like to, but I am not worthy." In response to the same question of who determined her unworthiness, she too said, "I did."
>
> A member mother who had known for many weeks that her daughter had planned a temple marriage was asked if she was going to attend the temple ceremony. "No. I am not worthy to get a temple recommend," she answered.
>
> Each of these people seemed to have made his own determination about worthiness. We do not have to be hindered by self-judgment. All of us have the benefit and added wisdom of a bishop and a stake president to help us determine our worthiness and, if necessary, to assist us to begin the process of becoming worthy to accomplish whatever goal we wish to achieve. When we take it upon ourselves to pass self-judgment and simply declare, "I am not worthy," we build a barrier to progress and erect blockades that prevent our moving forward. We are not being fair when we judge ourselves. A second and third opinion will always be helpful and proper.[2]

How wonderful and how wise this counsel! If we really, seriously think we should not take the sacrament we should first counsel with our priesthood leaders. We should never self-judge as to our worthiness—either to take the sacrament or go to the temple. Often as bishop, I would determine that participation in these ordinances was the very thing I wanted my members to do, even if they were not fully perfect. It was the healing and motivating aid they needed. To hold this back, in certain circumstances, could be counterproductive. Stephen Robinson once gave this helpful advice: "Many of us are trying to save ourselves, holding the Atonement of Jesus Christ at arm's distance and saying, 'When I've perfected myself, then I'll be worthy of the Atonement.' But that's not how it works. That's like saying, 'I won't take the medicine until I'm well. I'll be worthy of it then.'"[3] Such an idea is crazy and laughable. It's also very dangerous.

The word *worthy* is an interesting one, especially as it is used in the Greek in the New Testament. The most common usage of the word *worthy*, especially as it is used in the context we are discussing, is *hikanos* (transliteration), which simply means "sufficient," "enough," or "sufficient in ability" (see Matthew 3:11; Luke 7:6; 2 Corinthians 3:5). In this context, *worthy* does not mean one is perfect—it means they are sufficiently obedient or humble. A scripture is worth noting in this regard: "And when I had said this, the Lord spake unto me, saying: Fools mock, but they shall mourn; and *my grace is sufficient for the meek*" (Ether 12:26; emphasis added). In other words, worthiness is not a function necessarily of perfection, it is a function of where our heart is!

To be sure, there are certain levels of comportment that the Church expects and has defined, especially for temple recommend interviews, and these should always be met. However, as a bishop dealing with a struggling young adult, I often found that as soon as they were pointed in the right direction, as soon as they were humble and sincere, I would almost immediately, without fail, strive to get them to the temple and the sacrament table. These were the medicines of Christ's healing and atoning powers.

The Seven Blessings of the Temple

President Gordon B. Hinckley observed, "I know your lives are busy. I know that you have much to do. But I make you a promise that if you will go to the house of the Lord, you will be blessed, life will be better for you."[4]

During my life I have grown to love temples and temple work. I have had experiences, too sacred to share, that convince me the work that is performed therein is real and efficacious. I have come to know, as President

Hinckley has taught, that our lives are and will be blessed because of our being in God's Holy House. Although there are many blessings that come from temple attendance and participation, I would like to mention seven blessings (seven Ps) that I have personally discovered in my life.

(1) Peace

The temple is a place of peace. It exudes a feeling of peacefulness outwardly, even from a distance. Inside the temple, this feeling is amplified in very real ways through the subtle, gentle presence of the Holy Ghost. Furthermore, it's a place where individuals go and learn how to live lives of peace, rooted in the gospel of Jesus Christ. Finally, the temple is a place we go to labor vicariously for the deceased in order to bring peace to their lives as well. President Thomas S. Monson has given this wise reminder:

> As we attend the temple, there can come to us a dimension of spirituality and a feeling of peace which will transcend any other feeling which could come into the human heart. We will grasp the true meaning of the words of the Savior when He said: "Peace I leave with you, my peace I give unto you. . . . Let not your heart be troubled, neither let it be afraid."
>
> Such peace can permeate any heart—hearts that are troubled, hearts that are burdened down with grief, hearts that feel confusion, hearts that plead for help.[5]

(2) Power

The temple is a place of power. The Lord said to the Saints in the early part of this dispensation, "Wherefore, for this cause I gave unto you the commandment that ye should go to the Ohio; and there I will give unto you my law; and there *you shall be endowed with power from on high*" (D&C 38:32; emphasis added). This scriptural and revelatory allusion to the Kirtland Temple that would soon be built was complimented with this clarifying insight just a few days later: "And inasmuch as my people shall assemble themselves at the Ohio, *I have kept in store a blessing such as is not known among the children of men*, and it shall be poured forth upon their heads. *And from thence men shall go forth into all nations*" (D&C 39:15; emphasis added). It is worth noting the connection between "power" being given to the Saints and missionary work, or going "forth into all nations." This pattern of bestowing power with a purpose is followed today with many of the Lord's servants preparing to go forth into the vineyard, or who are preparing to enter into the covenant of eternal marriage. Power is bestowed in the temple not just to gratify our ambition. No, it is given for the sole purpose to build God's kingdom in homes and lands throughout the world.

Elder David B. Haight has taught: "A temple is a place in which those whom He has chosen are endowed with power from on high—a power which enables us to use our gifts and capabilities . . . to bring to pass our Heavenly Father's purposes in our own lives and the lives of those we love."[6] In the Doctrine and Covenants, the Lord has said: "Yea, verily I say unto you, I gave unto you a commandment that you should build a house, in the which house I design to endow those whom I have chosen with power from on high" (D&C 95:8).

A feeling of power comes to one the moment they step into the precincts of the temple. In the dedicatory prayer of the Kirtland Temple, Joseph Smith, assisted with this revealed prayed, made this poignant plea for those that enter into the house of the Lord:

> That thy glory may rest down upon thy people, and upon this thy house, which we now dedicate to thee, that it may be sanctified and consecrated to be holy, and that thy holy presence may be continually in this house;
>
> And *that all people who shall enter upon the threshold of the Lord's house may feel thy power*, and feel constrained to acknowledge that thou hast sanctified it, and that it is thy house, a place of thy holiness. (D&C 109:12–13; emphasis added)

(3) Protection

The temple is a place where we gain protection. This protection can readily be seen and is often associated with the wearing of the temple garment. It should be understood that the garment of the Holy Priesthood is not just "magic underwear" as some scoffers claim. This "promise of protection [inherent in the receiving and proper wearing of the garment] is conditioned upon worthiness and faithfulness in keeping the covenant."[7]

Furthermore, it is sometimes claimed that the temple garment gives some sort of physical protection from fires, falls, freakish accidents, and a whole host of other unfortunate mishaps. Perhaps such thoughts may be soothing and explanatory to some as they seek to explain the fortunate avoidance of certain perils they have encountered in life. We should respect their opinions and experiences. But let us be clear what the Church and its leaders teach as to the "type" of protection that the temple garment really offers.

The fundamental principle ought to be to wear the garment and not to find occasions to remove it. . . .

The principles of modesty and keeping the body appropriately covered are implicit in the covenant and should govern the nature of all clothing worn. *Endowed members of the Church wear the garment as a reminder of the sacred covenants they have made with the Lord and also as a protection against temptation and evil.* How it is worn is an outward expression of an inward commitment to follow the Savior.[8]

President Thomas S. Monson further described this protection: "As we go to the holy house, as we remember the covenants we make therein, *we will be able to bear every trial and overcome each temptation.*"[9] No, this protection is not magical nor mystical. It comes as we remember covenants and as we keep them. This is the protection that the temple garment can give us as we wear it appropriately and with purpose throughout our lives.

(4) Perspective

The temple gives us perspective. It focuses our hearts and minds not only on the things of eternity but likewise on the things that matter most, including and especially the Atonement of the Lord Jesus Christ. President Boyd K. Packer taught:

When members of the Church are troubled or when crucial decisions weigh heavily upon their minds, it is a common thing for them to go to the temple. It is a good place to take our cares. *In the temple we can receive spiritual perspective.* There, during the time of the temple service, we are "out of the world."

Sometimes our minds are so beset with problems, and there are so many things clamoring for attention at once that we just cannot think clearly and see clearly. *At the temple the dust of distraction seems to settle out, the fog and the haze seem to lift, and we can "see" things that we were not able to see before and find a way through our troubles that we had not previously known.*

The Lord will bless us as we attend to the sacred ordinance work of the temples.[10]

Likewise President Benson has counseled, "Temples are places of personal revelation. When I have been weighed down by a problem or a difficulty, I have gone to the House of the Lord with a prayer in my heart for answers. The answers have come in clear and unmistakable ways."[11]

(5) Purpose

The temple gives us a purpose. This purpose is often found in serving others and sacrificing of our time, talents, and possessions to build God's kingdom as we help build the lives of others through the restored gospel. Elder Oaks taught: "Hundreds of thousands of faithful members participate in the unselfish service we call 'temple work,' which has no motive other than love and service for our fellowmen, living and dead."[12] In this regard the Lord has said:

> For behold, I have accepted this house, and my name shall be here; and I will manifest myself to my people in mercy in this house.
>
> Yea, I will appear unto my servants, and speak unto them with mine own voice, if my people will keep my commandments, and do not pollute this holy house.
>
> *Yea the hearts of thousands and tens of thousands shall greatly rejoice in consequence of the blessings which shall be poured out,* and the endowment with which my servants have been endowed in this house. (D&C 110:7–9; emphasis added)

(6) Preparation

The temple prepares us for many things, especially celestial glory. President Monson reminds us that "in the temple, the precious plan of God is taught. It is in the temple that eternal covenants are made. The temple lifts us, exalts us, stands as a beacon for all to see, and points us toward celestial glory. It is the house of God. All that occurs within the walls of the temple is uplifting and ennobling."[13]

(7) Perseverance

Finally, the temple gives us the blessing of perseverance. In simple terms, it is a place where we go that helps us and enables us to endure to the end. It gives us strength and ability to go on through our lives.

> And one of the elders answered, saying unto me, What are these which are arrayed in white robes? and whence came they?
>
> And I said unto him, Sir, thou knowest. And he said to me, *These are they which came out of great tribulation, and have washed their robes, and made them white in the blood of the Lamb.*
>
> Therefore are they before the throne of God, and serve him day and night in his temple: and he that sitteth on the throne shall dwell among them.

They shall hunger no more, neither thirst any more; neither shall the sun light on them, nor any heat.

For the Lamb which is in the midst of the throne shall feed them, and shall lead them unto living fountains of waters: and God shall wipe away all tears from their eyes. (Revelation 7:13–17; emphasis added)

I am convinced that this ability to endure and persevere comes because we have chosen to make the decision that all must make if they are to return to Father's presence one day, that is "they have washed their robes, and made them white in the blood of the Lamb." Ultimately the only way back to Heavenly Father's kingdom is through the atoning sacrifice of the Savior. We find that all we do in the temple, all that we see, all that we say, all that we experience—all of it together points our souls symbolically to Christ and His salvation, which makes eternal life possible.

Notes

1. Dallin H. Oaks, "'Judge Not' and Judging," *Ensign*, August 1999.
2. Marvin J. Ashton, "On Being Worthy," *Ensign*, May 1989, 20.
3. Stephen E. Robinson, "Believing Christ," *Ensign*, April 1992, 9.
4. Gordon B. Hinckley "Excerpts from Recent Addresses of President Gordon B. Hinckley," *Ensign,* July 1997, 73.
5. Thomas S. Monson, "Blessings of the Temple," *Ensign*, May 2015, 91–92.
6. David B. Haight, "Come to the House of the Lord," *Ensign*, May, 1992, 15.
7. Letter to priesthood leaders, October 10, 1988; as found in Carlos E. Asay, "The Temple Garment," *Ensign*, August 1997.
8. Ibid; emphasis added.
9. Thomas S. Monson, "Blessings of the Temple," *Ensign*, May 2015, 93; emphasis added.
10. Boyd K. Packer, "The Holy Temple," *Ensign*, February 1995; emphasis added.
11. Ezra Taft Benson, "What I Hope You Will Teach Your Children about the Temple," *Ensign*, August 1985.
12. Dallin H. Oaks, "Unselfish Service," *Ensign*, May 2009, 93.
13. Thomas S. Monson, "Blessings of the Temple," *Ensign*, October 2010, 13.

About the Author

C. Robert Line has worked full time with religious education for the past twenty-five years. In addition to teaching with the BYU Religious Education faculty, he has been a presenter at BYU Education Week, Women's Conference, and Especially for Youth and has worked for Church Educational System programs as an instructor and director for Institutes of Religion. Brother Line has both a bachelor's and master's degree from BYU and also holds a doctoral degree from Purdue University in

sociology of religion. He has authored various books and articles and has served as the editor in chief of *Century Magazine*. Brother Line has served in the Church as a bishop, stake high councilor, elders quorum president, and various other callings. He played on the BYU men's basketball team from 1984 to 1985. He and his wife, Tamera Wright Line, have five children and six grandchildren. Their family resides in Cedar Hills, Utah.

Scan to visit

www.crobline.com